DREAM GUIDE

An Unofficial Guide to Walt Disney World - 50th Anniversary Edition

by Adam Hattan

The *Hattan* Company

The *Hattan* Company

Hattan Co.
PO Box 759
Banbury
OX16 6PQ
United Kingdom

© 2020 The Hattan Company Ltd.

ISBN: 978-1-9160897-3-0

For information about custom editions, special sales, premium or corporate purchases, please contact The Hattan Company Ltd. at contact@adamhattan.com

DREAM GUIDE

An Unofficial Guide to Walt Disney World - 50th Anniversary Edition

by Adam Hattan

Whilst every effort has been made to ensure the content of this book is accurate, over time this information will become out of date. For this reason, please consult with your travel agent or with Walt Disney World directly for updated information on shows, attractions, dining locations, merchandise offerings, prices etc.

The publisher cannot accept responsibility for changes, errors or omissions in information provided within this book or for the consequences of any reliance by users on the information provided within this book.

Reviews and advice on particular elements of a visit to Walt Disney World including but not limited to attractions, shows, dining locations and resort hotels are those based on the authors own experience and opinion. Your experience may differ from those described within this guide.

You're welcome to write to the publisher to share your feedback on this issue or ideas/suggestions for future issues.

Hattan Co.
PO Box 759
Banbury
OX16 6PQ
United Kingdom

CONTENTS

INTRODUCTION

For millions of people around the globe, Disney offers an escape from the real world. Whether it's for the length of a movie, song, television show or theme park attraction, Disney has a special ability to help us dream a little bit more than we're used to. Walt Disney World gives us a destination to escape the real world and live amongst our wildest dreams.

I'm lucky enough to have worked in Walt Disney World for two years, holidayed there in my teens and now visiting the resort is a huge part of my job. For most people, Walt Disney World is a once in a lifetime destination. This means not everyone gets the chance to master the parks, spend all their time wisely, find the best dining locations or find out the hidden secrets of the resort.

Having enjoyed days upon days in the parks, hotels and surrounding areas as both a guest and cast member, I've done the leg work for you. You won't need to spend your time or money learning the hard way!

On October 1st 2021, Walt Disney World will be celebrating it's 50th anniversary! With this, I wanted to not only update my first edition but also celebrate the fact that Walt Disney World has been making dreams come true for 50 magical years. The resort has grown a lot since it's debut in 1971 and even more so in the last few years.

This special 50th anniversary edition of my Dream Guide, is a consolidation of my years of experience in and around the resort, with some new magic thrown in. From the addition of Star Wars: Galaxy's Edge to the new Disney's Riviera Resort, there's a lot of new magic to explore and I've got the tips and tricks to help you do it well.

With my experience, I'll walk you through from beginning to end, helping you plan the ultimate holiday from the comfort of your home. Not only that, I've designed this guide in a way that makes it a little more tailored than other guides out there. I'll recommend hotels, dining and attractions based on what you actually like and want! Additionally, I'll hand you some extra-special tips, tricks and lesser known facts of the resort.

Walt Disney World is where I've had the pleasure of growing up, it's where I discovered my passions in life and lived out my wildest dreams. Disney means the world to me and Walt Disney World is somewhere I really consider a home away from home.

Whether you're planning your 1st or 51st visit, it's my wish that this guide will hold your hand and show you everything you didn't know you needed to know. Kick back and relax, I'm here to bring the knowledge directly to you and ensure your next trip to Walt Disney World is as magical as can be.

- Adam Hattan

Dream Guide is here to advise you and your family, specifically based on your demographic, likes, dislikes and priorities. Each section of Dream Guide is divided up into the different stages of planning and enjoying your Walt Disney World holiday.

Within each section, I've provided information tailored to all manor of family units. So whether you're a singleton, adult couple or family of 10 or more, you'll be able to find the tips and tricks that will make your holiday special. To make Dream Guide as simple as can be, I'll be using some rating systems and handy icons to help you find what's right for you quickly and easily.

It's Written in the Stars

Throughout Dream Guide, you'll find these star ratings. These will help me communicate my priority rating for each element I'm discussing. Sometimes they'll be related to a specific subject (e.g. a hotel's location) or they'll show you whether a particular attraction is a must-do or a 'if we have time' kinda thing.

One Star

Don't think for one moment that one star means it's terrible. It just means that based on my experience, your time may be better spent elsewhere.

Two Stars

At a two star rating, I don't want to discourage you from trying it as it may be right for you but in my experience, it's not on my list of priorities.

Three Stars

Three stars indicates that it's worth your time. See if you can make time for this but if you miss it, it's something you can do next time.

Four Stars

You'll want to make time for this. Having experienced most of what Walt Disney World has to offer, this is one of my favourites.

Five Stars

An absolute must-not-miss or one of my best recommendations for your trip! I don't hand out five stars for just anything.

One Size Does Not Fit All

You and your family are all individuals! You all have your own interests, likes and dislikes. However, when it comes to family units, space and suitability is one thing we can all agree is important on a holiday. For that reason, the below family unit icons will help you navigate what is likely suitable for you.

Single Adult

Having travelled on my own to Disney on a number of occasions, these are my recommendations if you're flying solo.

Adult Couple / Adult Friendship

Whether you're having a romantic getaway or going away with a friend, these will offer some great magic for you.

Honeymoon Couple

Whether on your actual honeymoon or a dedicated romantic retreat, these recommendations will have a little more flair.

Adults with Children

No matter how old your little ones are, these recommendations will give you some high quality family time.

Large Family

If you're taking the parents, the kids, the grandparents and the kitchen sink, these recommendations will work for you.

Grandparents / Experienced Adults

If you're bringing your parents/grandparents or you're an 'experienced adult,' these options may suit a steadier pace.

Single Parent

Regardless of age, if you're taking your little one away by yourself, these recommendations should work well for you.

Attraction Icons

On-Ride Photo

Choose these attractions if you're looking to put Disney Photopass to good use (page 94).

FastPass+

These attractions are FastPass+ enabled, meaning you can book a fastpass return time (page 73).

Money, Money, Money

A trip to Walt Disney World is not cheap, there's no secret about that. There are however ways to visit Disney without breaking the bank. If you're willing to be mindful about your spending before and during your holiday, you can avoid coming home with a crazy credit card bill. Use the below icons to be mindful of how certain activities may effect your bank balance.

Lower Cost

If you make an effort to use these options throughout your trip, you're less likely to have a heart attack when you see how much you've spent. Using dining as an example, these meals should cost less than $20 per adult.

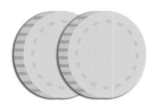

Average Cost

These options will be pretty common within the guide. They'll be the typically affordable destinations within your holiday. Using the same dining example as above, you'll be looking at approximately $40 per adult.

Higher Cost

Higher cost options are tailored for those not looking to hold back and those looking for a special treat within their holiday. Using the dining example, expect to spend anything upwards of $60 per adult.

Weather

Florida is one of the most unpredictable climates in the world. Within just a few minutes it can go from gorgeous sunny weather to something out of a disaster movie. The weather can be difficult to navigate when you're trying to stick to a plan or you're not sure what you're looking for. These icons will help you decide on attractions and dining locations that will suit the current weather.

Sunny & Warm

Consider this as your 'all systems go' indicator. If this is next to something, it's my recommendation that this location is best enjoyed with warm or clear weather.

Hot & Humid

Florida can get dangerously hot. It's with this, you'll find recommendations that give you a chance to get out of the heat and cool down a little.

Thunder Storms

Thunder storms may be cool but they're incredibly dangerous and arrive regularly in the Orlando area. If you see this symbol, you'll know that it'll work for you in the very worst weather.

Rain

If it's not a thunder storm you're in for, expect to at least see some rain. These recommendations will help you dodge and prepare for wet weather during your stay.

Chapter 2
YOUR HOME AWAY FROM HOME

Walt Disney World really is a world! With over 25 onsite resort hotels, in all manor of price brackets, it's easy to get a little overwhelmed by the choice. However, I'm here to help you narrow your options.

Prices for each resort change per the time of year and their availability. We can, however, start off by getting you a few ideas of where you might like to stay. Disney categorises it's hotels into three main tiers: Value, Moderate and Deluxe. First we'll take a look at the benefits of an onsite hotel and then dive into the tiers to find you some great options!

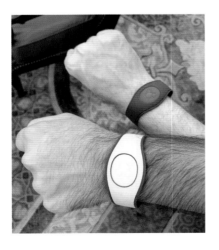

The Magic's in the Band

One of the greatest benefits of staying in a Disney resort, is this little band. If you choose to stay onsite, everyone in the family get's their own MagicBand! You can even choose the colour and it's labeled with your name.

This seemingly simple band makes your holiday so much more enjoyable and saves you carrying a lot with you! Just look at all it can do:

- If utilising Disney Magical Express service, you'll use your band to check-in.
- Your hotel room door magically opens with just a tap of your MagicBand.
- Your MagicBand can be linked to a credit/debit card. This saves you from having to carry your wallet and gives you the freedom to pay for meals, merchandise and snacks whilst out and about. Don't worry, you have to enter a unique pin for each purchase, so there's security in place to make sure no one else can use your MagicBand if you were to loose it.
- It also has your park ticket, photopass, and FastPass+ information linked to it. This allows you to do everything from enter the parks to adding your on-ride photos to your online account. All with just a tap!
- If you choose to purchase a Disney Dining Plan, this information is also linked to it. This means that at a table service meal, all you need to do is scan your MagicBand and sign the receipt. At a quick service location, it's just a tap.

Let Disney Do The Driving

From the moment you arrive at Orlando International Airport (MCO), Disney has all the transport taken care of. With a Disney resort reservation, you have the ability to add Disney Magical Express to your reservation at no extra charge. Magical Express is a transfer service from MCO to your Disney resort hotel. Whilst it makes a couple of other resort stops along the way, it's free and saves you the cost of a rental car/taxi as well as the hassle of driving in unfamiliar territory.

Disney is equipped to get you anywhere on property, free of charge. Disney's bus, boat, monorail and Skyliner services get you as close to the main entrance as you can get! If you choose to park a car, you've got the added journey from your car to the front of the park, as well as the added cost of parking (currently $25).

FUN FACT

The Planet Hollywood restaurant in Disney Springs, whips up more than 5,000 milkshakes each month!

Stay in the Magic

An added benefit of staying in Disney is you're never not wrapped in Disney's outstanding guest service and exceptional theming. No matter where you are on your holiday, Disney will be taking care of you the whole time.

You're also close to all the fun! If you've been to Disneyland Paris or Disneyland Resort in California, you might be thinking 'oh we'll just save our money and stay near-by.' Slight problem with that however, no other resort is 'close' to the Disney parks in Florida. Disney owns some 30,000 acres (the same size as the city of Chicago), which means only Disney resorts are within a 15 minute journey of the attractions. Some hotels are close enough to walk to one of the theme parks or even Disney Springs.

Extra Magic Just for Disney Hotel Guests

Two major benefits that allow you to experience some of the best attractions in Walt Disney World are early booking for Fastpass+ and Extra Magic Hours during your stay.

Fastpass+: Disney is great in that they offer complimentary priority access to a wide selection of popular attractions in each theme park. Most theme parks around the world will charge you for this service! In Walt Disney World however, if you're not quick enough when booking your free fastpasses, you may be left without fastpasses for your must-dos! By staying in a Disney resort (and some select neighbour hotels), you'll get to book your fast passes 60 days in advance. 30 days ahead of those with park tickets only. I'll let you know a little more about the booking process later on in the guide (page 73).

Extra Magic Hours: Every day during your Walt Disney World trip, Disney will open a park early or close it late, just for Disney resort guests! As soon as Extra Magic Hours begin, you'll have to scan your MagicBand to prove you're staying on property. The benefit of this is that it reduces wait times for some of the most popular attractions and frees up some breathing space!

PRO TIP

Extra Magic Hours don't always equal quiet time. If anything, parks with EMH on any given day, tend to be busier! Sometimes it pays to go to another park without EMH for the normal opening time.

How to Choose a Disney Resort

Choosing a hotel can sound like a daunting task. Fear not however, I'll walk you through the different price tiers, give you my honest opinions of each hotel and share whether I think they're right for you.

Try creating a shortlist of three or five resorts as you go through. This will give you options when you come to actually booking your trip.

Whilst reading through the price tiers, be mindful of the following tips:

★ Whilst a value resort should in theory be cheaper than a moderate resort, there are some exceptions to the rule. I'll explain when we come to booking later on but always compare a couple of hotels and room types, I wouldn't ever just pick and book.

★ Getting carried away at this stage could ruin your holiday. It's exciting choosing your hotel but know your budget and stick to it. Spending too much on a room that you're not using all day everyday, may take precious pennies away from your other experiences.

★ Know how and where to book. I'll show you how to book your Disney holiday in the best way to ensure you get the best price (page 53).

What's actually at a Disney resort?

Sure, Disney resorts have some great benefits attached to them but what's really there? You may be spending a number of weeks at this resort! Here's a breakdown of what's featured at all Disney resorts; regardless of price tier.

⭐ **Swimming Pool**: Most Disney resorts feature a themed pool and a 'quiet' pool. Around the main pool during the day, the kids activity cast members will be there to entertain your little ones should you choose to bask in the Florida sun (just be sure to supervise them). Quiet pools don't tend to 'close.' As long as you're respectful of the rooms nearby, you could quite happily enjoy a late night swim.

⭐ **Arcade**: Sometimes the only thing that will keep the little ones quiet for 30 minutes is arcade games. Just load up a game card and let the kids (and big kids) play until their heart's content (or until they run out of points and come crying for more).

⭐ **Laundry Facilities**: As much as we all try to avoid it, you may need to wash some clothes whilst on holiday. Every resort features washer and dryer facilities as well as vending machines with detergent.

★ **Quick Service Dining**: Quick service refers to fast food. Whilst your mind may jump straight to burgers and chicken nuggets (which they do serve), you may also find 'make your own pasta' bars, sandwich stations, bakeries and special selections tailored to the resort theming. e.g. Mexican specialties at Disney's Coronado Springs.

★ **Parking**: If you choose to rent a car when you arrive at Orlando International Airport, parking is available at all on-site hotels. However, there are parking charges to consider. For value resorts this is $15 a night. The price increases to $20 a night at moderate resorts and $25 a night at deluxe resorts.

★ **Bus Station**: No matter which resort you choose to stay at, they all feature a bus station to take you to every park, Disney Springs and the water parks (sometimes an in-direct service).

★ **Merchandise**: Disney will always make sure you've got plenty of opportunity to purchase your souvenirs. Some resort shops are better than in the parks!

★ **Bar**: Don't worry parents, there's alcohol not too far away if it all gets a bit much. Whilst these may be a basic pool bar, most bars offer a varied menu and excellent service.

PRO TIP

The drinking age in the state of Florida is 21 years old. Cast members are required to request ID of anyone they think may be around or under 30 years of age. Have valid ID on you! UK travellers, be sure to read page 93.

Value Resorts

Value resorts tend to offer you the best of both worlds if you're used to staying off Disney property. They won't wring you dry of every penny but they will open the door to all the benefits only Disney guests get to enjoy.

Of course, these resorts aren't the best of what's on offer at Disney but you'll likely find these hotels go above what other external hotels offer.

All value resorts grant you access to the on-site benefits such as Extra Magic Hours and complimentary Disney Transport. However, I'll make sure you're not compromising on magic whilst you try to save some money.

Benefits of Value Hotels

★ Cheapest resorts for a standard two queen bed room.
★ Ample number of rooms so it's often easier to book a stay (if doing so in advance).
★ Hugely family-friendly! With their quirky theming, kids love value resorts.
★ Affordable family suites are available at value hotels, so you can be together whilst also enjoying plenty of space.

What Disney Won't Tell You

★ At certain times of day, buses will service multiple resorts. This means bus rides may take longer and it may be difficult to get a seat.
★ The rooms cover what you need but not always what you want.
★ These hotels will often host tour groups and larger group bookings. As such, the rooms are often more used than others and there may be some noise disruption.
★ Not the best theming in my view.

1. Disney's Art of Animation Resort

As the newest value resort hotel, Art of Animation is well maintained, fresh and a whole lot of fun to stay at! Featuring mainly family suite room combinations in Finding Nemo, Lion King and Cars themes - this is a great place to stay with a family of 4 or more. There's also a whole lot of photo opportunities.

Because of the room combinations, this resort will often be more expensive than other value resorts. However, with space for up to 6 people in the suites, it's often cheaper than booking two rooms. Linked with Pop Century (below) the resort now offers a Skyliner service to Epcot and Hollywood studios. I've stayed here multiple times and never been unhappy.

BEST FOR	VALUE FOR MONEY	LOCATION

      ✦ ✦ ✦ ✦ ✦   ✦ ✦ ✦ ✦ ✦

2. Disney's Pop Century Resort

ADAM'S CHOICE - If you're looking for the value resort that offers you the most for your money, look no further than Pop Century. With the resort themed with oversized icons from the 60's through to the 90's, this is great for nostalgia! This resort also benefits from not being too big. No matter where your room is, it won't take you long to get to the bus station, Skyliner or quick service.

The resort benefits from recently refurbished rooms that consolidate space. One of the double beds folds away to provide extra floor space and a dining table. Ideal for solo travellers or couples who prefer sharing a bed.

I love this resort for when it's just myself or if I'm bringing a friend. The only downside is that as it's a fan favourite, availability is very patchy. You may want to consider booking this one as far in advance as you can. If you get the chance to visit, even whilst staying elsewhere, be sure to get the chocolate chip pancakes! Honestly, one of the best quick-service breakfasts on property.

FUN FACT

Before Art of Animation was built, that land was going to be used for an early 1900's expansion of Pop Century. Construction was halted after the decline in travel in 2001. Disney then realised, the early 1900's were no longer relevant to most guests.

BEST FOR

VALUE FOR MONEY

✦ ✦ ✦ ✦ ✦

LOCATION

✦ ✦ ✦ ✦ ✦

3. Disney's All Star Resorts

If you're looking for the cheapest stay possible, you'll likely find All Star Music, All Star Movies or All Star Sports to be your best option. These three resorts are basically one big resort split into three different themes. Each separate theme has its own quick service, bus station, pool etc. Consider these resorts for a last minute trip as when there's availability, you can get an amazing deal here!

The All Star Resorts are favourites for large tour groups. If there's a cheerleader convention when you're planning on being in town, you may find a lack of availability or a higher rate per room. The bus routes will also sometimes take you to each resort. Making what would be a 10 minute taxi ride to Disney Springs a 45 minute journey on a pretty packed bus.

The savings are great here and you do still get the perks of being 'in Disney' but for me, if you're not planning on using the on-site perks to the max, you may find similar hotels for cheaper off property.

BEST FOR	VALUE FOR MONEY	LOCATION
👥👨‍👩‍👧👩‍👧	✦ ✦ ✦ ✦ ✦	✦ ✦ ✦ ✦ ✦

Moderate Resorts

Moderate resorts are often the best you can get for your money. They offer more than value resorts but won't charge enough to bankrupt you.

Whilst moderate resorts aren't as close to the parks as Deluxe resorts, they're certainly closer than the value resorts and offer extra transport services that make your holiday a little more comfortable.

Moderate resorts also offer you that extra level of theming; going beyond something quirky to something atmospheric.

Benefits of Moderate Hotels

⭐ Best price for the amenities and comfort you can achieve from a Disney resort.
⭐ Multiple bus stops mean you're never too far away from a bus to the parks.
⭐ A little more is on offer in the way of food and evening entertainment.
⭐ Looking for a themed room? Well you're in the right place! Whether you want to be pirates or royalty, there's a room for that!

What Disney Won't Tell You

⭐ Depending on which bus stop you're closest too, you may have to wait for a couple of buses.
⭐ Moderate resorts are the larger resorts and so it may be a walk to the food locations, main pool etc.
⭐ Because of their popularity, availability at these resorts is few and far between in peak seasons.
⭐ Due to bodies of water, mosquitoes are a common irritant.

PRO TIP

When booking a moderate resort, I recommend making a request or two. Once you've received your reservation confirmation, give Disney/your agent a call and ask to add a request to your booking. This could be anything from a ground floor room for Grandad, or for your room to be close to the main area for a shorter walk to the bus and food court in the mornings. Disney will always do their best to accommodate your request. However, please note they're not guaranteed.

1. Disney's Fort Wilderness Cabins

This resort offers the magic of Disney but the escape of a wilderness campground! You can easily spend a chilled out day here forgetting you're even in Walt Disney World. Fort Wilderness celebrates the classic American aesthetic you may have seen in The Parent Trap (1998).

Fort Wilderness is by far one of my favourite resorts! It's a great place to just enjoy time with friends/family. So even if you don't end up staying here, do stop-by for dinner or an afternoon of recreation. The resort offers some of the best 'beyond the parks' activities you'll find.

Why not take your little one on their first pony ride, paddle a canoe down the bayou or take a wagon ride before you adventure to the Hoop-Dee-Doo Musical Revue (country dinner show)! There's so much to do here, you'll have to visit a number of times to see it all. Hoop-Dee-Doo is great for a special occasion or to mix-up your holiday routine. It's a dinner show where you and your family get to feast on an all-you-care-to-enjoy (and drink) dinner whilst clapping, singing and laughing along to the country inspired show.

If you can't afford the dinner show this time, be sure to go for dinner next-door at Trail's End. An all American buffet featuring pot roast, cowboy beans, corn bread and strawberry shortcake! If you're looking for a cheap evening, head to Chip and Dale's campfire. Here you can get a Smores pack to roast marshmallows by the fire ($10), sing and dance with Chip and Dale before enjoying a Disney movie on the big open air screen (FREE).

The cabins at Fort Wilderness offer you the benefit of being together, with the added perk of space! Cabins feature a kitchen, lounge and family bathroom. You'll have more than enough space to relax after a day in the parks.

BEST FOR	VALUE FOR MONEY	LOCATION

FUN FACT

Disney still has permission to build a Nuclear Power Plant in Walt Disney World, having been grated permission in 1967. However, Disney has no current plans to utilise this permission and has instead built multiple solar energy farms.

2. Disney's Port Orleans - Riverside

ADAM'S CHOICE - If there was one resort that was the best value for money, in my eyes it's Port Orleans - Riverside! Whilst not technically a deluxe resort, I always perceive it as one. For the amount it offers, matched with the level of theming and pure quality, it's something special. You could even treat yourself to a Royal Guest Room for an extra magical stay. These themed accommodations offer a room that has been decorated for Disney royalty; kitted out with the subtleties that make it the most 'Disney' room you'll find at Walt Disney World.

PRO TIP

Looking for the ultimate evening of romance? Consider a horse drawn carriage ride at Port Orleans. Maybe also get some beignets from French Quarter.

Riverside hosts one of the best evening entertainments with the singing piano man on select nights each week. It has one of the best kid-friendly pools and possibly the best quick service restaurant in Walt Disney World! Additionally, you'll be able to use a boat service to Disney Springs for shopping and dining. My advice is to request a room close to the main area since it is a big resort. It'll make the walk back a little more enjoyable.

BEST FOR

VALUE FOR MONEY

✦ ✦ ✦ ✦ ✦

LOCATION

✦ ✦ ✦ ✦ ✦

3. Disney's Port Orleans - French Quarter

Sister resort to Port Orleans - Riverside, French Quarter offers similar location in that it's close to Disney Springs but there are some cuts you have to take if you choose to stay here over Riverside. This is only in consideration of that it's often the same price as Riverside but has less choice in amenities. The resort, however, benefits from a newly refurbished quick service, cafe and Jazz lounge. It's a favourite of families that are looking for that small-town vibe and if you like beignets, look no further!

The resort's styling embodies the culture and architectural style of New Orleans. Whilst I believe you get more for your money over at Riverside, there's something to admire in the cobbled streets that make up the walkways around the resort. The resort is ideal for knowing your little ones are unlikely to loose their way back to the room, thanks to the resorts more compact layout.

BEST FOR   **VALUE FOR MONEY**   **LOCATION**

4. Disney's Caribbean Beach

If you've ever looked at booking via Virgin Holidays, you've probably seen that this resort comes up as the best price for a moderate resort. For that reason, it's British holiday maker central! As it's so popular with us Brits, it'll normally fill up if there's a promotion going, such as free-dining (page 69).

Having most recently undergone a complete overhaul, the resort now benefits from a more practical layout, new restaurant, new quick service and is the main hub for the Disney Skyliner. Whilst the Skyliner is a massive benefit of this resort, there are some compromises. In order to accommodate the new layout, Imagineers had to scale back the size of the merchandise shop and quick service. I personally think you can get more for your money elsewhere (in terms of room design, food offerings etc.) but it is a fan favourite with many regular guests.

BEST FOR	VALUE FOR MONEY	LOCATION

5. Disney's Coronado Springs

Out of all the Disney hotels I've stayed at, this one exceeded my expectations the most. Having a similar layout to Caribbean Beach, I always assumed this would be the same... It isn't! The hispanic theme that runs throughout the resort is fantastic and the newly refurbished rooms are as if you're staying at a deluxe resort.

Since the opening of the new Gran Destino Tower, there's plenty of choice when it comes to dining, snacking and drinking. There's also a fantastic new lobby that could put some deluxe resorts to shame! The pool is certainly one-of-a-kind and the amenities of this resort make it a close contender for 'Adam's choice', if not beat it on the sheer number of offerings. This resort also benefits from being slap-bang in the middle of Disney property, so it doesn't take long to get anywhere.

BEST FOR	VALUE FOR MONEY	LOCATION

Deluxe Resorts

It's time for the best of the best! Now I warn you, if you're looking to stick to a strict budget, stop reading now. Disney knows what luxury looks like and they make sure their deluxe resorts are themed and priced as such.

If money's no object on your next Walt Disney World holiday, this is certainly the section for you. With above and beyond service standards, signature dining and rooms that'll make you question whether or not you're dreaming, you're sure to have a once in a lifetime experience staying in one of these.

Benefits of Deluxe Hotels

★ Each deluxe resort is located next to one of the four theme parks (sometimes they're even walking distance).

★ Club Level (extra charge) offers you a step beyond just luxury with concierge service, complimentary snacks, drinks and food.

★ Astounding resort theming.

★ Perfect for a romantic getaway or you can just pop-in to feel fancy for an evening.

What Disney Won't Tell You

★ They're very expensive! You'll often see the deluxe resorts on TV but not everyone can afford the high nightly room rate.

★ Whilst close to one park, they're often a long way from the others.

★ Unless you know what you're doing, you could pay a lot of money for a not-so-great room.

★ Expect to pay through the nose if you're looking for anything more than just a two queen room.

FUN FACT

Before the Grand Floridian was constructed, the plot of land was initially slated to be occupied by an Asian inspired resort. Not only that, Disney had plans to extend the monorail track beyond the Contemporary and alongside Bay Lake to build a deluxe Persian inspired resort.

1. Disney's Grand Floridian Resort & Spa - (Magic Kingdom Area)

If you're looking for the ultimate in Disney luxury or you want the best of the best in club level service, look no further than the Grand. This Victorian style resort boasts monorail service to the Magic Kingdom (just one stop away) and boat service directly back from the Magic Kingdom. Whilst the price is a little out there, it sure is luxurious!

The Grand Floridian for me is the 'treat-yo-self' resort. Mainly as the average cost exceeds $500 per night for two adults. However, if you're looking for a way to make a stay here more affordable, consider booking last minute. On occasion, Disney will run some incentive offers (e.g. 20% off summer bookings).

Rooms are most commonly two queen beds but within the resorts Disney Vacation Club building, you may find villas that can sleep up to 10 people.

If you choose to upgrade to Club Level, my advice is to pay the extra to stay in the Main Building. The Main Building Club Level overlooks the lobby and allows you to enjoy the evening band and pianist from the comfort of your private lounge - with snacks and drinks on tap.

BE SURE TO VISIT - Even if you're not staying here, there's so much to see and do at this resort, it's worth a visit. You could enjoy a five diamond dining experience at Victoria & Albert's, enjoy the live pianist and band that alternate from 4pm everyday, enjoy a drink in the Enchanted Rose bar or even take a pontoon out on the Seven Seas Lagoon. You won't want to miss the chance to indulge yourself without the cost of a night's stay. Just bear in mind the pool and Club Level lounges are for guests of the hotel only (unless you choose to book a spa treatment, in which case you get access to some resort amenities.

BEST FOR

VALUE FOR MONEY

LOCATION

2. Disney's Polynesian Village Resort - (Magic Kingdom Area)

Drift away to the elegant land of Polynesia. With the essence of Hawaii in it's theming and dining offerings, Disney's Polynesian Village has a great atmosphere about it. The resort boasts one of the best family style restaurants (Ohana) and is the only place outside of Magic Kingdom where you can get a refreshing Dole Whip. You'll even get a lay when you check-in!

I stayed at the Polynesian for a night and whilst the room was delightful, the things I wanted to do and enjoy were all outside of the room. For example, I wanted to watch the Fireworks from the beach, get a Dole Whip, hang out at Trader Sam's or explore the lobby. All things I could've done without paying the nightly room rate. You'll likely pay a similar price here to that of other Magic Kingdom resort hotels. This is the resort I wouldn't stay at myself but would definitely visit for one evening.

FUN FACT

Around Walt Disney World are a number of fountains that guests throw loose change into. Disney actually collects this money and donates it to central Florida charities.

I know a number of families that make this their go-to because they enjoy spending so much time at the resort.

If you choose to stay here, my advice would be to request a room either close to the beach or main lobby. It's bigger than you think.

BEST FOR   **VALUE FOR MONEY**   **LOCATION**

3. Disney's Contemporary Resort - (Magic Kingdom Area)

Not every hotel has a monorail running through the atrium! If you've been to Walt Disney World before, there's little chance you missed this hotel! Renowned for it's unique architecture and contemporary style, if you're looking for simplistic luxury, the Contemporary may be for you.

This is the one deluxe resort I have not stayed in, simply because to get a room in the tower, you'll be paying a small fortune. It's never been affordable for me to stay even one night here, let alone a whole trip. Don't be looking to stay here if you're on a strict budget is all I'd say. I know that once you've stayed here though, it'll very quickly become your home away from home (from what I hear).

BEST FOR

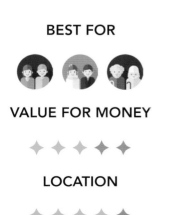

VALUE FOR MONEY

LOCATION

4. Disney's Wilderness Lodge - (Magic Kingdom Area)

If you love the idea of cuddling up in a cabin, high in the mountains; Wilderness lodge is the place for you! With a wooden masterpiece lobby and a mountainous American inspiration, this resort is something truly unique. Surrounded by gorgeous woodland, you'll be forgiven for thinking you're in northern California.

This resort has the benefit of being close to Magic Kingdom without the feeling of being in a high traffic area. Slightly off the beaten track and looking onto Bay Lake, this is a resort that's popular for it's natural beauty. With a fantastic pool and lakeside bar & grill, you'll be able to feel at one with your woodland surroundings.

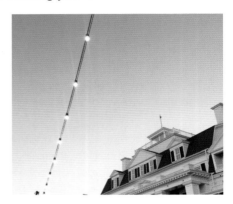

BEST FOR	VALUE FOR MONEY	LOCATION

5. Disney's Boardwalk Inn - (Epcot Area)

Are you a night owl? Well the Boardwalk is the place to be! Known for it's close proximity to Epcot via International Gateway (the back entrance) and it's vibrant nighttime scene, the Boardwalk uses a turn-of-the-century theme to make you feel as though you're staying along a Victorian pier.

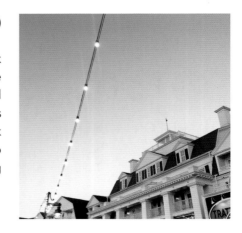

This is also a great resort to visit, even if you're not staying near-by. The Boardwalk has dining, entertainment and bars open until late. The pool is fun for kids with it's carnival theming and the rooms offer class, whilst also being playful. My only criticism with this resort is that it charges more per night than other hotels with better theming and facilities. E.g. neighbouring Yacht and Beach Club. I'd certainly say this is a more grown-up resort if you were thinking of staying here.

BEST FOR	VALUE FOR MONEY	LOCATION

7. Disney's Yacht & Beach Club Resort - (Epcot Area)

ADAM'S CHOICE - Love swimming? Look no further than the Yacht and Beach Club! This twin hotel features the Yacht Club (themed to nautical luxury) and the Beach Club (themed to fun at the seaside); with both resorts sharing a water park! This is the only pool on property featuring a lazy river, it has the tallest water slide out of all the on-site hotels, it has a sand bottom pool and two hot tubs! If you enjoy the seaside and water, you'll be right at home here.

I personally prefer the Yacht Club resort for it's more mature offerings and styling. It has two luxury restaurants; The Ale & Compass and one of my favourite on site restaurants; The Yachtsman Steakhouse. Beach Club does a great job of hosting families with their character buffet Cape May Cafe and the famous ice cream parlour: Beaches and Cream. Here your family could take on the 'Kitchen Sink Challenge.' Ordering a kitchen sink will have lights flashing and the cast members shouting as they bring over your 8 scoops of ice cream, every topping in the house and a whole can of whip cream (A WHOLE CAN?!).

BEST FOR	VALUE FOR MONEY	LOCATION
	✦ ✦ ✦ ✦ ✦	✦ ✦ ✦ ✦ ✦

PRO TIP

When checking into your Disney resort, I recommend asking if they have any 'complimentary upgrades available'. Sometimes when there's relatively low occupancy, cast members may have the opportunity to reallocate your room with a better view. This of course isn't guaranteed but can sometimes mean you get a little extra magic without paying anything more.

8. Disney's Animal Kingdom Lodge - (Animal Kingdom Area)

Escape to the savannahs of Africa at one of my favourite Walt Disney World resort hotels. Disney's Animal Kingdom Lodge offers you a destination resort whilst also being close to the fun of Animal Kingdom theme park. African culture has always been interesting to me but here it truly comes to life in the level of detail Disney has employed throughout the dining locations, rooms and theming.

It's one thing to see a Giraffe walking by your window but it's another to hear African drums played by African nationals hosting you at the hotel. Disney's Cultural Representative Program allows African nationals to come to the hotel and work in the resort, giving you a chance to learn about their culture whilst staying in the magic of Disney. This resort also benefits from being a little further afield than most deluxe resorts. It may take you a little longer to get to Magic Kingdom or Disney Springs, but you benefit from being able to escape the hustle and bustle when you want to relax at your hotel.

There's something about this resort that makes it stand out above the others to me. The food, the cast and the atmosphere is so transportive, it has another layer to it than just being a 'Disney' hotel. It creates magic in reality and not just in fantasy. Here, I can genuinely forget I'm in Florida and just enjoy the peaceful surroundings. This is another resort I highly recommend visiting for an evening.

BEST FOR

VALUE FOR MONEY

LOCATION

PRO TIP

Animal Kingdom Lodge is great for a first time deluxe stay, as it's more affordable when booking a standard view. If you do book this view, call and kindly request for a partial savannah view (it's included in this room rate).

DVC Resorts

DVC stands for Disney Vacation Club. I won't dive too deeply into what it is but it's essentially a long-term time-share offering from Disney.

DVC has been very successful for Disney over the years, so much so that they've created purpose built resorts for DVC members. However, you're still welcome to book these resorts, providing there's availability.

These properties are villa resorts. Meaning they're designed for families that are likely to be sharing accommodations and cooking some of their own meals. Whilst most DVC villas are built into the previously listed deluxe resorts, these next three resorts are purpose built.

Benefits of DVC Resorts

★ They offer more spacious accommodations that feature kitchenette's and washer/dryers.
★ Often more affordable to share a villa with a large family than it is to get several standard rooms in a deluxe resort.
★ Exceptional resort theming.
★ A more family vibe, since most people staying in these resorts have been multiple times to the same DVC resort.

What Disney Won't Tell You

★ Availability is few and far between as DVC members get priority in booking these villas.
★ Compared to similar layouts elsewhere on property (e.g. Art of Animation) these villas are very expensive at a rack rate.
★ The older DVC resorts are pretty dated.
★ These resorts tend to be further away from the parks than standard deluxe resorts.

1. Disney's Old Key West - (Disney Springs Area)

Opened in 1991, this is by far the oldest DVC resort. Whilst the resort is probably in need of a major overhaul from an outsider perspective, it brings the same families back year after year. I personally would compare the theming to a seaside retirement village but I know plenty of people disagree with me. If you're looking for a more Florida feel, this is probably the resort for you.

BEST FOR

VALUE FOR MONEY

✦ ✦ ✦ ✦ ✦

LOCATION

✦ ✦ ✦ ✦ ✦

2. Disney's Saratoga Springs - (Disney Springs Area)

Similar to Old Key West, Saratoga Springs is more for the repeat visitor that calls Saratoga home. The theme of this resort is carriages, horse stables and the like. For me, you can find much better theming for the same price elsewhere on property but if you want to spend a lot of time shopping and eating, this is the only resort in which you can walk directly to the Marketplace at Disney Springs.

BEST FOR	VALUE FOR MONEY	LOCATION

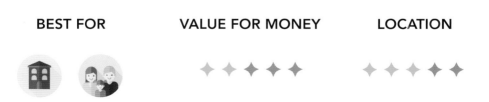

3. Disney's Riviera Resort - (Epcot Area)

If there's one resort that's moved to the top of my Disney bucket list, it's this one! With easy access to Disney's Hollywood Studios and Epcot via the Skyliner, I could see this resort becoming my favourite in the near future. With direct access to two theme parks and Magic Kingdom and Animal Kingdom equal distance away, this resort is all about three things: location, location, location.

Disney are definitely looking to modernise their luxury styling and Riviera is a big step in the right direction. Mirroring the style of other five star resorts (e.g. Four Seasons), Riviera Resort is something unlike anything else on Disney property. I highly recommend visiting Topolino's Terrace on the top floor for an exceptional character breakfast or fine dining evening meal.

Inspired by Walt Disney's love of European architecture and the French Riviera, this new resort blends spectacular room design with elegant food from across the pond. This resort marks a new milestone in Disney's evolution of the Disney Vacation Club product, in creating a dedicated DVC resort that rivals some of the staple deluxe hotels across property.

BEST FOR	VALUE FOR MONEY	LOCATION

Club Level

If you're looking to upgrade your Walt Disney World stay even further, you may want to consider staying in a club level room. Currently, club level is available in all deluxe hotels, as well as Gran Destino Tower at Disney's Coronado Springs.

Club level is essentially a dedicated part of the hotel (normally a separate floor) that allows guests to have a more seamless check-in experience via a dedicated concierge desk, access to complimentary snacks and drinks throughout the day, turn down service and a concierge team that will go above and beyond to make your stay as magical as can be. Whilst you'll be paying a much higher nightly rate, these services do make your stay very special indeed.

Is it right for me?

I would only recommend paying for club level if you were looking to make a shorter stay extra special and you wanted to spend a lot of time in the resort. I personally don't see the value in spending so much extra per night for access to the food/drinks/service if you were going to be out in the parks for most of your stay. I'd say, this would be a great idea for a honeymoon trip.

Benefits of Club Level

★ Ability to book fast passes 90 days in advance.
★ Dedicated concierge team to assist in getting you dining reservations, event tickets etc.
★ Snacks and drinks (including alcohol) served most of the day.
★ Truly exceptional service standards that will make it hard to go back to standard rooms.

Off Property

Whilst staying on Disney property is my personal preference, it's sometimes a lot more affordable to stay off Disney property in a near-by hotel or possibly a villa. If you're considering staying off property, here are my tips for finding your home away from home.

Villa or Hotel?

My family and I have stayed in villas and hotels and in my experience the hotels have added much more value to our stays. You might be thinking that a villa is the only option if you're taking more than five people but it's not necessarily the case. There are plenty of hotels with suites, of which will comfortably host up to 10 people. It all depends on your preferences.

Tips for Staying in a Hotel

- There are a multitude of hotels near Walt Disney World and thus the competition for price is always hot in the area. You're more likely to find a killer deal by choosing to stay in an off-site hotel if you book smartly.
- Take a look at the included services and the location of the hotel. Free transport to the parks and being close to popular restaurants, are huge helps in making your off-site stay more enjoyable.
- If you choose an official neighbour hotel of Disney (e.g. the hotels in the Disney Springs area) you can still get access to some of the on-site perks like being able to book fast passes 60 days in advance.
- Hotels are notorious for having hidden charges (like resort fees). Do some digging and weigh up all the costs before choosing to book a good rate.

Tips for Staying in a Villa

* If you're travelling with a large group, a villa may be the most affordable option if you're all wanting to stay together and are booking in advance.
* Fresh food isn't always cheaper from the supermarket. Most fresh produce has to travel to Florida so don't be surprised to find fresh meat, fruit and vegetables more expensive than you'd expect.
* Research the area. Just like anywhere, there are safer places than others. Whilst the price of a villa may be a steal, it's important to check where your villa will be. Your safety is something that can't be compromised for price.

Do Your Research!

Whether choosing to stay in a hotel or a villa, it's paramount that you do your research. Read reviews, check out the local area on Google Maps and find out how long it'll take for you to get to each park. The last thing you want is a 45+ minute drive back to your hotel/villa after a 10 hour day walking in the hot Florida sun.

Don't Tighten the Purse Strings Too Much

Whilst you're shopping hundreds of options, it's important to remember that not all hotels/villas will make for a dream holiday. Whether you think it or not, you will be spending a lot of time at your accommodation. One of my biggest tips is the need for rest time. You want to feel comfortable in wherever you choose to stay. For that reason, I wouldn't make my hotel or villa the first compromise if it came down to price. It may be one of the biggest costs but it could make or break your trip. I speak from experience when I say I've gone for the 'do the job' accommodation and instantly regretted it on arrival.

Chapter 3
WHICH TIME IS YOUR TIME?

When you consider Walt Disney World is open 365 days a year and there's an abundance of annual festivals and special events, it's sometimes difficult to decide when you'd like to go. Maybe you want the weather that suits your family's preferences or perhaps you're looking for the most affordable time of year?

I'm sorry to say that choosing your time to go is a never ending list of ifs and buts. Ultimately, it comes down to what YOUR priorities are. That's how I've designed this part of Dream Guide. Start with your priority, whether that's being there for a special event, for the best weather, for the lowest crowds or for the cheapest time of year.

Choose the priority that's right for your travel party and turn to the relevant page. There I'll give you the best tips for your wants and needs.

WEATHER

Florida seems to work on two seasons rather than four. Winter and Summer. If you're travelling December - March, expect it to be chilly some days. Whilst it's unlikely you'll see frost, you'll likely need a jacket with you. April - November is basically summer. Expect hot days and warm nights. Because of these two extremes, choosing to go in the transition period, means you're more likely to get some nice temperatures and less likely to encounter disruptive rain.

Don't worry about dates of travel just yet. I'll help you when we get to booking to make sure you get the best deal for the time of year you're looking at. For now, work out which month you'd be interested in travelling.

If you consult the graph on the right, you'll see when temperatures may be more to your liking. If I've rated a month 5 - be aware it'll be very hot and very humid! If you're traveling from northern states in the US or the UK, chances are you won't mind the lower temperatures.

If you want to bake to a crisp, June - September is most definitely your time. On the next page, check out some of my best advice for the time of year you're considering with pros and cons.

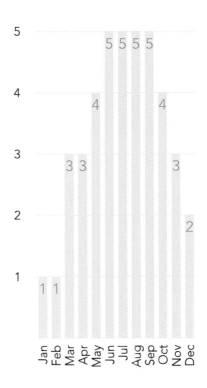

January - March

If the cold never bothered you anyway, you're looking at the right time of year. Not only that, you'll be able to take advantage of some slightly lower crowds compared to other times in the year.

Tips for January - March

★ If you love Epcot, or you've never been and would like to experience Epcot at it's very best, look out for dates of Epcot's Flower & Garden festival. Typically starting towards the end of February, it's a great opportunity to see World Showcase on a whole other level. The festival features multiple speciality food stalls, beautiful Disney character topiaries and colourful gardens everywhere.

★ If you love art and don't mind going as early as January, check dates for Epcot's Festival of the Arts. You'll have the chance to step into artwork and try food & drinks that have a special artistic flair.

★ Spring break is the second busiest time of the year at Walt Disney World. Whilst Spring Break dates vary per each state, check dates for states within driving distance of Florida. This is when the resort will see the biggest increase in guests. Spring Break tends to run February - April.

Pros for January - March

★ There's fewer people in the parks compared to other times of year.

★ Great Epcot events throughout the season (check Disney's website for up-to-date information & dates).

★ Thanks to less demand, you can get some great deals during these months.

Cons for January - March

★ The parks often prioritise repairs and construction during this time of year. Don't be surprised if there's a crane topping up the paint on Cinderella's castle.

★ Watch out for Feb/March as this is Spring Break season. It's very busy during this period.

★ It can be bloomin' cold.

April - June

Possibly the best time of year for goldilocks weather! Not so hot your shoes melt into the asphalt but not so cold you'll need to bring a coat. I've found the best weather during April and May specifically.

Tips for April - June

★ Especially in April/May, this is one of the rare times in the year that you can enjoy the heat without the humidity. This nice weather is no secret however, so expect it to be reasonably busy around the Easter holidays.

★ May is a good time for experiencing the parks at their best in my opinion. Reasonable crowds, nice weather and some pretty good deals normally.

★ It's around this time of year Disney will open their new attractions and shows.

Pros for April - June

★ Perhaps the best weather out of the entire year.

★ As the parks prepare for their busiest season, you'll often find most attractions are free from routine refurbishment.

★ If you avoid the national and local holidays, it's often not too busy.

Cons for April - June

★ With Easter and a number of national holidays in these months, it's tricky to dodge all busy times.

★ Schools in the US tend to break-up for summer around May-June time so the crowds will pick-up.

★ Prices will be higher around national and local holidays.

July - September

It's getting hot in here! Summer is in full swing during these months and I warn you, it's not for the faint hearted. With temperatures often exceeding 32c (90f), 100% humidity on most days and thunderstorms almost every day, it's not the most comfortable time of year.

Not only is the weather sometimes torture, US and UK schools are out for summer which makes the parks consistently busy and prices for hotels and park tickets go up significantly.

Tips for July - September

- ⭐ Summer is no longer the 'busiest' time. Whilst not quiet, you'll still have a great time!
- ⭐ When booking for these months, either book 12+ months in advance or last minute.
- ⭐ Be prepared for extreme weather and insure your trip against cancellations due to hurricanes.

Pros for July - September

- ⭐ June is normally the month new attractions will aim to open by. As such, you could be one of the first people to experience the latest addition to Walt Disney World.
- ⭐ Late August/early September, is quickly becoming the quietest time of year in Walt Disney World.

Cons for July - September

- ⭐ It's hot! Too hot!
- ⭐ On-the-day park tickets are priced based on how busy the season is. If you're travelling domestically within the US, be prepared for these prices.
- ⭐ Regular thunderstorms will cause some attractions to close often.
- ⭐ Did I mention it's too hot?

October - December

This is the season for more events than you can shake a stick at! With Mickey's Not So Scary Halloween Party, Epcot's Food & Wine Festival, Mickey's Very Merry Christmas Party and Epcot's Festival of the Holidays all in this season, there's more than enough to make your visit during these months something special. These months are great if you've been to Disney before and you're now looking for something to make this trip different from the last.

Tips for October - December

★ Florida's hurricane season runs until November. Insure your trip and be ready for hurricane disruption.

★ Book special ticketed events ASAP. These events can sell out quickly.

★ Dodge the major holidays to avoid spending more than you bargained for. You can also find some sweet spots that aren't as busy this way.

Pros for October - December

★ The weather is a little kinder day to day (temperature wise).

★ There will always be something special to do. Whether it's Halloween or Christmas, you'll be incredibly entertained (for a price).

★ You'll likely get the chance to see some amazing fireworks!

Cons for October - December

★ Christmas is the busiest time of year for Walt Disney World. Don't be too surprised if most resorts are sold out. Book in advance to avoid being disappointed.

★ If you time it wrong, you could be in for an incredibly busy time.

PRICE

Money, money, money. It makes the world go round and unfortunately, a lot of what we plan for our Walt Disney World holidays is based on our budget. It's pretty common for price to be the biggest priority in making a trip to Disney viable. As I go to Walt Disney World more often than the typical family, I've learnt a thing or two about making a trip affordable. From how/where/when you book, through to saving whilst on your trip, hopefully I can save you a pretty penny.

The Cheapest Time to Go

Let's not beat around the bush here, the cheapest time to visit Walt Disney World is late January through to mid February. It's not rocket science; the weather is colder, people have less money after the holidays and thus there's fewer people visiting. To keep visitors coming during this time, the prices for hotels will drop. As long as you can A: be flexible enough to go during this time, B: don't mind it a bit chilly and C: can deal with a couple rides being closed for refurbishment, this is your time.

Whilst winter may be the cheapest time of year, it's not ideal for everyone. For that reason, I'll take you through some dos and don'ts when it comes to prioritising price for your Walt Disney World holiday. It's not practical for me to put prices in Dream Guide as they'll likely be out of date by the time it goes to print. For that reason, use my tips to choose your ideal time based on current availability and pricing.

Best Price Realisations

If you're looking to go to Walt Disney World for as cheap as possible, there are some harsh realities I have to impart.

★ You cannot go to Walt Disney World in the school breaks cheaply. If you've got little ones and you need to go out of term time, your best bet is a half-term break when the American schools are in session.

★ It's a gamble getting a good deal on a holiday like this. You need to have a little faith (trust and pixie dust) that when you find a good price, it's worth the leap of faith to book when you see it. If you wait a day or two, things will likely change and it'll be gone.

★ There's a lot of compromises involved in booking for the best price. You likely won't be able to achieve your once-in-a-lifetime trip on a tight budget, just because Walt Disney World is expensive for the average family.

★ If this is your first time going, consider a time when there are no big holidays. That way, you get to see the resort as a blank canvas. You'll save a little money and give yourself something to do next time to make it different.

★ Someone else, may be able to get a better price than you. As stubborn as I am in finding the best price, sometimes a tour operator or travel agent can access special rates and thus save you a lot of money.

PRO TIP

If you want to get your holiday for the best price and still travel in high season (e.g. Christmas), try and hold out booking until closer to the time. About 90-30 days before your intended arrival, you can find some decent prices on flights and hotels as the resorts try to secure their occupancy going into the high seasons. The only problem is that there is no guarantee your preferred hotel (or any) will have availability. Be sure to check often!

First Holiday on a Budget

If you're dreaming of your first trip to Walt Disney World and you're a little restricted on price, don't be too quick to book something when it comes into your budget. Do your research to make sure it's a resort you'll enjoy and check what the additional costs may be (e.g. parking & tickets). Your first time needs to be magical and if you're staying in a dive off-property, it won't be magical.

Book Ahead and Save

For most people, the most affordable way to book a Walt Disney World holiday (especially the first one) is to book over a year in advance during an offer. About Spring/Autumn time, Disney gives guests the chance to get free-dining if they book in advance during this offer. If booked far enough in advance, you'll only have to pay a deposit, then you've got time to pay it off. It could make an expensive trip more achievable when you've got time to plan out your payments.

FUN FACT

In Muppet Vision 3D at Hollywood Studios, Mickey Mouse makes a cameo at the end of the show. This was actually the first time Mickey Mouse appeared in a three-dimensional form.

CROWDS

There's a common myth that there are quiet times to go to Walt Disney World. Well, I'm sorry to be the bearer of bad news but this just isn't the case. Not at a specific time anyway. Walt Disney World is the most visited tourist attraction in the world and so you're never going to find a time when you can walk on every attraction. However, there are times you can avoid to ensure you're not waiting over an hour for every attraction you want to go on.

Typically, the rule of thumb is avoid the American national holidays. Any times like Spring Break, Easter, Labor Day, Thanksgiving, Christmas or New Years Eve, draw in the largest crowds. It's also around these times you'll often see the highest prices. Why would you want to pay more for your holiday and get on fewer attractions? Especially if it's your first time visiting the resort? As such, if it's your first time, consider a break that may avoid these peak times.

PRO TIP

If you end up in a park and it's busy, stick to the right hand side of the walkways as most Americans instinctively walk on the right. As such, you'll make more progress walking with the tide. When it comes to lines (e.g. quick service restaurants, security etc.) choose the line furthest away. Also, check how dense the line is and whether there's lots of large families. Larger families take longer to organise, slowing down the line.

To help you get a better visual understanding of the crowd levels throughout the year, I've created the following chart. This is a rough guide and should be treated as such, as dates and days of holidays change year on year. Each period has been ranked from 1 to 5 to show how busy it's likely going to be. 1 being lowest crowds and 5 being the highest.

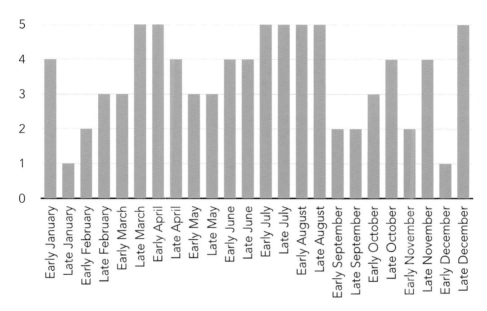

EVENTS

Walt Disney World knows how to celebrate! If you're looking for the ultimate Halloween party or maybe you're just looking for something to make your next holiday different from the last, Disney has you covered. Throughout the year, Disney hosts a variety of events that cater for many different interests. Whilst the dates of these events tend to change year-on-year, I've done my best to let you know when they are and what they entail. For ticketed events, read page 194.

New Year's Eve

If you're looking to ring in the New Year with a bang, know that Magic Kingdom, Epcot and Hollywood Studios all like to put on a pretty spectacular celebration. Whilst it's the single busiest night of the year for all the parks, these firework shows are something to be marvelled! Epcot tends to be my go-to.

Valentine's Day

If you happen to be in Magic Kingdom for Valentine's day, you may have the chance to enjoy some extra touches. In years gone by, we've seen special meet and greets for the princesses to meet guests alongside their princes, decorations and themed treats.

Festival of the Arts

Hosted typically from the middle of January till early February, Festival of the Arts is an event that takes over Epcot's World Showcase area. During this event little ones can enjoy arts and crafts events, there are art themed seminars, artistic food, drinks and photo opportunities.

Epcot's Flower & Garden Festival

Running through most of spring, Epcot transforms into a gardener's paradise! With extravagant flower beds and impressive topiaries, the park doesn't get much prettier than during this event. Not only that, you'll find a variety of food and drink kiosks around the World Showcase!

Easter

If your little ones (or you for that matter) would love the chance to meet the Easter Bunny, head to Magic Kingdom on Easter weekend. The parade also features a special Easter pre-parade featuring Mr & Mrs Easter Bunny and a flurry of Easter inspired costumes.

4th of July

Whilst a little awkward for us Brits, this is the day that Americans celebrate their independence. 4th of July is celebrated by the mother of all firework displays. Whilst not one of my favourite displays that Disney do, if you're looking for a lot of ooh and ahh, this is a night for you.

Epcot's Food & Wine Festival

Typically running from September through to November, the festival brings a plethora of food and drink stalls to Epcot that allow you to taste your way (or roll your way) around the world. You'll find things you've never even heard of before and maybe see a band from way back when.

Mickey's Not So Scary Halloween Party - (ticketed event)

With event dates starting as early as August, this ticketed event turns Magic Kingdom into an exclusive Halloween party featuring a special stage show, Halloween parade and an awesome firework display! You can even dress up and go trick or treating.

Mickey's Very Merry Christmas Party - (ticketed event)

Christmas is one of my favourite seasons to visit Walt Disney World. At this special ticketed event, Magic Kingdom features a special stage show, complimentary cookies, the ultimate Christmas parade and a firework display that'll warm the heart of even the biggest Scrooge.

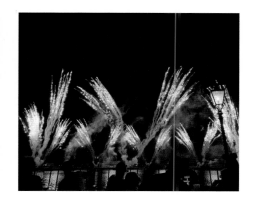

Epcot's Festival of the Holidays

Just in case you thought Epcot was lacking in festivals, there's more! During this event there'll be a special candlelight procession hosted by some pretty big names, beautiful decorations and the chance to hear each country's local holiday story. You could even meet Mr & Mrs Clause.

PRO TIP

Walt Disney World hosts a few marathon weekends out of the summer seasons. Whilst typically when the crowds are lower across the parks, marathon runners can sometimes book up the resorts very quickly. Check the dates in case you'd like to participate (paid event pass required) or you'd like to avoid them.

SCHOOL BREAKS

If you're travelling with little ones, chances are you'll have difficulty going outside of school holidays. For this reason, let me give you my advice for going during these breaks. Please note: this section will be in a UK format but should be a basic guide for other territories.

February Half-Term

If you're looking for a cheap getaway, this break could be perfect for you. Just note that by only going for a week, you'll likely have a more hectic schedule. Don't forget the kids will need to go back to school almost straight after you return. If you can, give them a couple days to recover.

Easter Holiday

Whilst you're likely to cross over with Spring Break, the weather is much more bearable during this period. Depending on the year, you may just avoid the worst of it. You'll likely be able to find a reasonable deal if you book far enough in advance. Just be sure to book your fastpasses and dining reservations.

Spring Half-Term

Providing it falls at the end of May, this will hopefully be the very best school break to take your little ones to Disney. Whilst restricted to one week, the crowds are moderate and you'll likely visit before the heat gets too much.

Summer Holiday

Things have changed in recent years that have made the Summer a better time to visit than others. Whilst prices will typically be higher than other times and it will be hot (very hot), crowds have shifted to later in the year. Since Summer became the time to avoid and October - December was coined as the best weather/low crowds, a lot of visitors have moved to this time of year.

If you're restricted to this break, go as early as you can. August and September are excruciatingly hot and have the most thunder storms. If your child maybe finishes before the majority of other schools (e.g. they finish their exams early) you can get a not-so-bad deal and avoid the worst of the heat. However, if it's as quiet as possible you're looking for and you can handle the humidity, leave it as late as you possibly can as American schools go back in mid-August.

Autumn Half-Term

If you want better weather and the chance to maybe experience Mickey's Not So Scary Halloween Party, this is the season for you. Just note however, the parks are considerably busier during this season. Non-party days at Magic Kingdom now have a reputation for being unbearable during this time of year.

Christmas Break

Christmas in Disney is beautiful with a certain charm in the air (amongst the over bearing crowds). Unless you can time your trip toward the beginning of December, I certainly wouldn't recommend the weeks around/over Christmas for a beginner. If you've done everything before though and know what you're in for, it might be a good time for you to visit.

Chapter 4
BOOK THE MAGIC

Now you've got some ideas of what you'd like your Walt Disney World holiday to look like, it's time to start making these dreams a reality. Hopefully by this point you've highlighted a hotel or two and you've got an idea of when you'd like to visit.

In this chapter, I'm going to walk you through the different booking methods to help you get everything you need, everything you want and for the best price!

There are no rules when it comes to booking your holiday. Some people like the comfort of booking a package and others are happy to book everything separately. Likewise, prices change so much, it's impossible for me to give you the perfect guide to getting the cheapest holiday year round. Before I get into showing you how to book, let's run over some 'need to knows.'

If this is your first trip to Disney, there's a lot of words and terminology that's floating about. Until now, you may not have understood them. Before you start using the booking methods to part with your cash, it's important to know what you want and what you don't. The last thing you want is saying yes to something you don't want or need and paying the price for it (literally).

DISNEY DINING PLANS

In short - it's a way to pre-pay for your meals and save between 5-10% over the course of your holiday (depending on whether you use it to the max).

However, don't get distracted by that discount. Disney Dining Plans (of which there's a few) are something you need to understand before adding one to your trip. The last thing you want is to actually have lost money by the end of your holiday.

How does the dining plan work?

When you book a Disney resort hotel and park tickets together, you'll be eligible to add a dining plan to your package. It's an all or nothing system. You either have the dining plan for everyone in your travel party for every night of your stay or not at all.

If you book the plan, you'll be allotted a number of dining credits (determined by the dining plan you choose) that you can use however you like.

For example, if you booked the 'Disney Dining Plan', you'd be allotted the following number of credits per person, per night of stay:

1 x Quick Service Meal (counter service)
1 x Table Service Meal (waiter service)
2 x Snacks (most food items around $5.00 in price)

Disney will tell you exactly which locations accept the dining plan but it's pretty much all of them. With a plan, you'll be given a re-fillable resort mug and be free to use your credits as you wish. At a quick service meal, you'll typically be able to get a meal and a drink. You'll scan your magic band and be given a receipt with a zero balance.

At a table service meal, you get one main course, one dessert and one drink (some alcohol is included for adults over 21 years of age). Anything you order outside of this allotment will need to be paid for at the end of your meal. You'll simply scan your MagicBand, sign a receipt and be given the opportunity to tip your server. You can pay your tip in cash or charge it to your room.

Is a Disney Dining Plan right for you?

There's a number of things to consider when it comes to choosing whether or not you'd like a dining plan. However, there's a rule of thumb I like to use.

Let's say you booked a dining plan, but chose to spend two or three days outside of Disney eating. Maybe you go to Universal Studios, the Florida Mall or even somewhere like Olive Garden. If you didn't use three table service credits and three quick service credits, you've wasted about $240 per person.

If you're planning on spending almost every day of your Walt Disney World stay in Disney, then the dining plan may be right for you.

However, it also depends on how much you and your family eat/drink. In my experience, if you're likely to have a cocktail, beer or glass of wine with every meal on holiday, the Dining plan is a great option. If you don't drink alcohol though and you're not big on snacking throughout the day, in my experience, you'd be better of paying as you go.

What's included on the Dining Plan?

How much you get per person and per night of stay, is dependant on the dining plan you choose. The below chart describes how many dining credits each guest gets per night of stay.

	Quick Service Dining Plan	Disney Dining Plan	Disney Dining Plan +	Deluxe Dining Plan
Re-Fillable Resort Mug	Length of Stay	Length of Stay	Length of Stay	Length of Stay
Snacks	2	2	2	2
Quick Service Meals	2	1	-	-
Table Service Meals	-	1	2	-
Choice of Quick Service, Table Service or Signature Restaurants	-	-	-	3

Notice that one of the plans is literally called 'Disney Dining Plan'. This may be referred to as the Table Service Dining Plan by some people and is considered the standard dining plan. It's also the most popular option.

Get the Most Out of a Dining Plan

I mentioned you could save 5-10% earlier. However, you'll only save that amount if you use your dining plan in full and wisely. If you don't use all your credits, you may as well have given Disney a stack of cash for no reason.

Not only is it important to use all your credits but it can also depend on where you choose to dine. Whilst most options will be priced similarly, there are places where you wouldn't get your money's worth. If your meal at a quick service will cost less than $13 per person, consider another option to get the best value for the cost of the plan. Likewise, if you're dining at a table service restaurant, choosing the cheapest thing on the menu every time and only getting soft drinks, you'd have been better off paying as you went. Just be mindful is all I suggest.

Tips for Using a Dining Plan

If you think a dining plan is right for you, here are some tips to help you use your Disney Dining Plan efficiently.

★ **Make Reservations** (where applicable) - if on the Disney Dining Plan or Deluxe Dining Plan, I strongly recommend booking a restaurant for each night of your stay. You can cancel them the day prior if you think you're unlikely to go (and avoid the $10 per person no-show fee) but when you're committing to a dining plan, it's a good idea to have something booked. Not having reservations may result in lots of waiting and/or disappointment.

★ **Play the Signature Game** - On the Disney Dining Plan, there are a select number of table-service restaurants that will take two credits per person. More often than not, these are Disney's 'signature dining' restaurants (places like Jiko, Be Our Guest and Cinderella's Royal Table). If you chose to dine off-property one evening (e.g. the mall or Universal Studios), you can use that saved credit to now dine at a signature restaurant. This is a great way to try the fanciest restaurants on property without paying the higher price of the Deluxe Dining Plan.

★ **Don't Forget About Tips** - When booking a dining plan, it's nice to get in the mindset of having everything paid for. However, your plan doesn't cover tips for servers. It's worth keeping that in mind when you come to budgeting your spending money.

★ **Use Your Snack Credits** - If come the end of your trip you have snack credits left, head to your resort merchandise location to stock up on treats that'll last the trip home. They can also double up as gifts for family and friends.

OFFERS

When it comes to booking a Walt Disney World holiday, there aren't really any offers that will make your holiday cheap. There are, however, options that'll allow you to get more for your money!

★ **Free Dining** - One of the best deals currently offered annually is 'free dining.' Available during select months, Disney will allow you to get free breakfast with a value resort reservation, Quick Service Dining Plan with a moderate resort reservation and Disney Dining Plan with a deluxe resort. Act fast when this offer activates as it's extremely popular!

★ **UK Exclusive** - Disney knows that UK visitors have more to pay in airfare and as such, UK residents can benefit from cheaper park tickets, earlier access to room availability and more. Check Disney's website for the latest.

EXTRA MAGIC HOURS

Extra Magic Hours (EMH) allow you to get an hour or two of bonus time in the theme parks. Only open to Walt Disney World (and official neighbour) hotel guests, you'll get the chance to enjoy the rides with far shorter lines.

Every day, Disney opens a park a little earlier or closes it a little later just for on-site guests. When you check-in to your hotel, you'll be given all the information of opening times, or you can view these times online and in the My Disney Experience app. If using Extra Magic Hours in the morning, you'll have your MagicBand scanned before being granted access to the park.

If Extra Magic Hours are after normal park closing, you'll need to scan your MagicBand with a cast member before entering the line of each attraction. Whilst Extra Magic Hours offer most attractions, it's worth mentioning that not all attractions will be open. Often the case in the mornings, some rides and shops will still be in the process of opening. For these attractions, save them for regular opening times.

Tips for Extra Magic Hours

⭐ **It's Exclusive** - If you're with friends or family that aren't staying in Disney, know that it's strictly for on-site guests only.

⭐ **Start Small** - Whether morning or evening, start Extra Magic Hours on the quieter attractions. The most popular rides will be busiest at the start.

MY DISNEY EXPERIENCE

The biggest mistake guests make before a Walt Disney World holiday, is not using and not familiarising themselves with My Disney Experience (MDE). It's a FREE app and area of the Walt Disney World website that enables you to manage your Walt Disney World stay.

Downloadable from the Apple and GooglePlay app stores, I highly suggest you download it at least 60 days before your holiday. As mentioned above, there is a website version if you don't have a smart phone or tablet. Here I'm going to explain what MDE is and how to best utilise it before and during your holiday.

What is My Disney Experience?

MDE is a one-stop-shop for all your Walt Disney World holiday needs. It's not that you 'can' use it but that you 'must' use it (to get the most out of your trip).

Within the app and online, you'll be able to link your Disney hotel reservation, link your park tickets, book fastpasses in advance, book dining, browse park maps, check opening times, check wait times for attractions, add items to your itinerary of must-dos and view your photos from photographers and rides!

It's only by having a Disney account (FREE) and using MDE that you'll be able to use the benefits available to you and use your complimentary MagicBands.

Can You Get Away with Not Using it?

In my opinion, no. Not using it will likely mean you miss out on the meals you wanted, waiting hours for rides and being a step behind most other guests.

Is it Difficult to Use?

Whilst not difficult, there are some tips and tricks to using MDE wisely. I'll give you the basics but Disney also provide a help desk and tutorials online.

Linking Your Information

When you first get started on MDE (in the app or online), you'll need to start by creating a Disney account if you don't already have one. Once signed in, you'll then need to go to the 'Friends & Family' section. Here you can add a profile for everyone that's coming on your trip (yourself included).

Once you've bought your park tickets and booked your resort reservation, you'll use the confirmation numbers to link them to your MDE account and build your holiday. **It's so important to link your tickets & hotel!** Without linking your tickets and hotel reservation within 60 days of your trip, you'll miss out on some of the best fastpasses.

I Need Help!

If you need to call the help desk, my advice is to call the moment they open. At the moment this is 1pm (UK time). Otherwise, you may be waiting a while.

FastPass+

Disney's Fastpass+ system is a digital reservation system for some of the most popular attractions. If you're staying in a Walt Disney World resort hotel, you'll be able to book up to three fastpasses per day of your trip, 60 days prior to check-in. If you're staying off property, you'll be able to book fastpasses 30 days prior to the start date of your park tickets.

These reservations will give you a one hour window to enter the selected attraction's Fastpass+ line. This will reduce your wait by up to 75%! All of this is managed through My Disney Experience either on the Walt Disney World website or via the My Disney Experience mobile application.

It's important to note, that in order to successfully book fastpasses on the first day possible (which I recommend), you must have your Walt Disney World room reservation linked to your My Disney Experience account and/or your park tickets. Then, on day 60, be on My Disney Experience from 8am EST (1pm GMT) to have the best chance of getting the fast passes you want for your trip.

When making Fastpass+ reservations, note that some attractions are split into different tiers. Meaning you'll only be able to book one fastpass in tier one, followed by two fastpasses from tier two.

If travelling from the UK and making a reservation with The Walt Disney Travel Company, just note it can take up to 10 days for your reservation number to come through. Meaning you should book your trip at least 70 days prior to arrival if you'd like to be able to book your fastpasses 60 days in advance.

Tips for FastPass+

⭐ **You can get more than three fastpasses** - Once you've used your three allotted fastpasses (and only when you've used them. This doesn't work if you didn't use one and the time has expired) you'll be able to book more fastpasses one at a time. Very few guests understand this which means you can often get multiple additional fastpasses throughout the day. Whilst it may be difficult to get the most popular attractions (as they're likely booked up), in somewhere like Magic Kingdom where most attractions are Fastpass+ enabled, you can save hours of waiting! You just can't book another fastpass until you've used the one you've already got.

⭐ **Book your fastpasses as soon as you can** - Because of some attraction's popularity, as soon as day 60 ticks over, you should be on MDE booking your favourites. When new attractions open, they'll always be the first ones to go. The last thing you want is to come to book your fastpasses and find out all the attractions you wanted are now gone. You're paying for this benefit so try your best to use it to the max. My advice is to start at the end of your holiday and work backwards, since fewer guests have access to the later days.

⭐ **Refresh, refresh, refresh** - Due to the amount of people using MDE at any given time, everyone using the system is seeing time-slots for attractions that are being held by the system for them. This means that one person booking their fastpasses has got up to three time-slots for every attraction in the park on hold whilst they choose which one they'd like to book. As soon as they've booked one, all those other time-slots are re-released. So, when booking your fastpasses, if you can't see the attraction you wanted or at a time that suits you, refresh your results a few times to check whether they're available.

⭐ **Book your fastpasses for earlier in the day** - As you can only book more fastpasses once you've used your allotted three, book as early as possible! The sooner you've used them, the sooner you can book more and with a better chance of getting some great attractions. As the day goes on, time-slots are obviously harder to come-by.

⭐ **If you miss your fastpass** - There is always the chance that you may be late to a fastpass. However, don't panic. As long as you're not more than 15 minutes past the end time, you'll be granted access. After that time, it's at the discretion of the cast member as to whether they'll let you through. Alternatively, you can modify that fastpass within MDE to be used on another attraction later in the day (providing it hasn't been used by anyone in your party).

⭐ **Check on the day** - On occasion, certain attractions will open more fastpasses to book on the day. Normally around mid-morning, if you look at modifying one of your current reservations, you'll be shown what's available. You could turn a 'meh' fastpass into a 'wow' fastpass on the day.

Dining Reservations

Booking your table service dining works similarly to that of FastPass+. The difference, however, is that you don't need to be staying on Disney property, or even have your holiday booked to get access to the reservations system.

If you have a Disney resort stay, dining reservations may be made for your whole trip 180 days prior to check-in. If you don't have a resort stay, it's 180 days in advance of each day. Most restaurants will have availability closer to arrival but for places like Cinderella's Royal Table and Be Our Guest, you'll need to book as soon as the reservations are released.

★ **Fees and cancellations** - Most restaurants are free to book. However, some may require you to pay in advance (e.g. Victoria & Albert's). Should you not turn up to a reservation, there's a $10 per person no-show fee. If you know you're not going to make a booking, cancel or modify it the day before to avoid getting charged the no-show fee. If something happens on the day out of your control, call the dining reservation line as they may be able to waive the fee in certain situations.

★ **Book as you go** - Because of the cancellation policy, a lot of people (and I mean a lot) will be cancelling the reservations they have for the next day. This means that you can often book some amazing restaurants during your trip. Even those that are highly sought after will pop-up during your stay. Be sure to check the app at least once a day to see what's available. In my experience, the best time to check is first thing in the morning (before 6:30am).

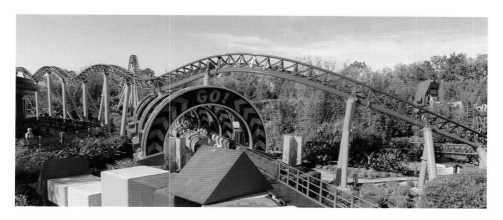

⭐ **Refresh, refresh and refresh again** - Just like fastpasses, the MDE system is constantly holding reservations whilst other guests choose the one they want to book. Keep refreshing the selections you've been given just in-case there's other times available or other dining locations you'd prefer.

Mobile Order

MDE isn't just great for booking table service dining. You can also order your quick service meals before you even get to the location!

Simply order ahead of your arrival via the Mobile Order service within the app. Once you arrive at the location, just click 'Prepare My Order' and within minutes you'll be told to collect your order from the collection window. It saves you lining up to pay for food and gives you some extra time to find a table.

Park Maps

Paper is out and digital is in! Whilst it was nice picking up a park map as a souvenir, the maps within the app can now show you exactly where you are and how to get to where you'd like to go. Not only that, you can view approximate wait times for attractions, saving you a walk to see if it's worth lining-up.

MagicBands

I mentioned earlier that you'll need to link your Disney resort reservation to book your fastpasses within 60 days. Once you've linked your reservation, head to the 'My MagicBands and Cards' section to customise your MagicBands ahead of your stay. You'll be able to choose a colour and the name you'd like printed for each person on your reservation.

MagicBands are finalised before you arrive. There's only a certain date up to which you can customise or modify your selections. If within the USA, your MagicBands will be sent to you. If travelling from abroad, you'll be given them when you check-in.

Opening Times & Bus Times

Within MDE, you're able to check opening times of the parks. This is especially helpful prior to booking your fastpasses as you can see which day you'll have Extra Magic Hours. Additionally, you can now see when the next bus is from your hotel. Simply navigate via the 'My Resort' button on the homepage.

Times Guide

Similar to park maps, you can check times for shows, characters and night-time spectaculars within MDE. Not only that, you can add them to your account plans to make sure you don't miss something.

BOOKING

Do It Yourself

If you're booking 10 months or less in advance and you're happy to do some leg work, I strongly recommend the DIY system. The following steps will walk you through how to best book a trip in parts and for the best price.

Step 1 - Don't Choose Your Dates

Hopefully you'll have an idea of when you'd like to go but whatever you do, try not to settle on specific departure and return dates before you've even started looking at prices. The key to this process is getting you the cheapest flights possible and flight prices vary day-by-day. If you're willing to be flexible with your dates, you may find yourself getting the deal of all deals!

Step 2 - Find Your Flights

I recommend using a flight comparison site like *skyscanner.net* to search flight prices for a particular month and then compare the different airlines. You can save soooooo much this way! Once you've had a look and narrowed down some dates, keep checking the prices for a week everyday. I say this because flight prices change day-by-day. If it looks like a steal and you can afford it, BOOK IT!

Step 3 - Check Hotels

Once you've either decided on your flights or booked them, it's time to start looking at hotels. Whether you're staying on or off property, start by using a hotel comparison site to have a good look at what's available. At this stage, it doesn't matter which hotel you've decided on. This will allow you to see all prices for all hotels in the near-by area. A great hotel deal could change all the plans you had.

By using the map tool on sites like *Hotelscombined*, *Trivago* etc. you can quickly browse in Disney and near Disney. Don't just book the cheapest, make a shortlist and research each one.

Step 4 - Book Your Hotel

Once you've chosen a hotel (Disney or non-Disney), get quotes from the hotel's website, a travel agent/tour operator, or the hotel's call center and consider the comparison site price. That way you'll know which booking method is right for you and/or the best price.

When it's a Disney hotel for example, I normally book through the Walt Disney World website as the price is often reflective of what you find elsewhere BUT you get the perks of booking through Disney. E.g. Having your booking handled by Disney, a welcome pack etc.

Step 5 - Dining Plan

If you choose to stay in Disney and would like to book a dining plan, know you'll need to book your hotel, park tickets and dining plan all together. For more information on what the dining plan is, how it works and whether it's right for you, go back to page 65.

Step 6 - Park Tickets

This should be the last big ticket item (see what I did there). I'm sorry to say tickets will never be cheap. With on-the-day tickets in excess of $120 per day, per person - it's important to book your tickets in advance and with certified sellers. Personally, I book tickets through the official websites. If you're in the UK, I promise you, tickets are the cheapest before departure (e.g. Disney's 14 Day Ticket). Not only do they include Memory Maker (page 94), they're heavily discounted (especially when there's an offer on).

Step 7 - Collate

With possibly everything booked in different places, it's important to print and collate all your booking confirmations in one folder.

Packages

If you're booking more than 10 months in advance, this will likely work best for you. When you want the booking process to be as care free as your actual holiday, a package deal can be the best way to achieve this. It's also what I'd recommend if you're set on having a rental car or flights aren't available yet.

Step 1 - Research

Even if you're set on a package deal, I recommend checking out the DIY method to booking (even if you just jot down an average cost of how much it'd cost to book everything separately). Going into booking your package with an idea of price, means you won't be taken for a mug when reviewing available packages.

Step 2 - Shortlist Some Package Holiday Companies

When it comes to package holiday providers, they're all very similar. If you're from the UK: Virgin Holidays, Tui, Ever After Holidays etc. are all selling the same Disney hotels, similar flights and similar rental cars. For that reason, open up a few website tabs, do your research and shortlist a few providers. Whilst all agents will be selling the same/similar products, it's going to come down to the service you receive and the holiday protection included, as well as the final price.

Step 3 - Check the Season

If you've already ran through the DIY process, you can go ahead and skip this step as you'll already have an idea of the cheapest arrival and departure dates.

Head to a flight comparison site like *skyscanner.net* and check out flight prices for the time of year you're looking at travelling (if flights aren't on sale yet, have a look at the same month in an earlier year). You'll be able to see if there's a particular date when prices go through the roof. This is particularly important when booking a package over or near school holidays.

Step 4 - Shop Till You Drop

Now it's time to make some phone calls. Whilst website prices are a good indicator, you'll only ever get the best price from an agent over the phone. Make your way through your shortlist and get quotes for the same dates, hotel and flights from the different travel companies. You'll then have an idea on who you'd like to book with.

Step 5 - Book it!

Prices are only temporary. Once you've got a good price with an agent/company you like, book it as soon as possible!

Chapter 5
KNOW BEFORE YOU GO

Walt Disney World is approximately twice the size of Manhattan island. Even after living there for two years, I still haven't seen and done it all! Whilst you won't be able to do everything in one holiday, I think it's good to know the basics before you arrive. In this chapter I've given you all the pieces of information I think are good for any visitor to know, prior to arriving in Disney.

1. You will not be able to do everything.

I repeat! You will not be able to do everything! The only thing you'll get from trying to do everything is sore feet and a grumpy family. Know that it's just not possible and you should instead try to treasure and really experience the rides, shops and restaurants you do get to see.

2. Getting from place to place takes time.

In Walt Disney World, getting about can take anywhere from 15 - 90 minutes. Disney transport is great but when busy times hit, it may take far longer than you expected to get from point 'A' to point 'B'. If you've got a dining reservation to make, I recommend giving yourself at least an hour to get there.

3. You're going to be walking a lot.

When you're in the magic of Disney walking from place-to-place, you'll soon forget how much you're doing. For that reason, it's a good idea to get yourself into walking before you leave for Disney and break-in any shoes you've bought for the trip. The last thing you want is blisters and foot ache on holiday.

4. There's more than burgers and chips.

A common misconception about Disney parks is that you'll be eating chicken nuggets, burgers and fries the entire time. Whilst you can certainly find these, every theme park and resort offers speciality food. In Epcot for example, you can literally eat your way around the world!

5. Adults can easily have a date-night.

Walt Disney World is not just for little ones. With outstanding fine-dining, bars and lounges, there's more than enough opportunity for a date-night unlike any other. With that in mind, select resort hotels have day-care and evening-care services to help the parents get a night to themselves. Even if you're not staying at Disney, these services are open to all guests (for a fee).

FUN FACT

Each holiday season, Walt Disney World uses more than 1500 Christmas trees across property.

6. Construction is always happening.

Walt Disney World is the number one tourist destination in the world. It doesn't stay that way by staying the same. No matter when you go, you will most-definitely come across a couple of attractions under refurbishment, new attractions being built and/or some routine maintenance.

7. It will be busy.

Whilst you may have visited a local theme park on a day when every ride was a walk-on, those days are few and far between in Walt Disney World. No matter when you go, you're likely to experience some busy days in the parks. Use unofficial crowd forecasts to plan which parks are likely best for each day.

8. Wi-Fi

Whilst within the theme parks, hotels and Disney Springs, you'll have access to Disney's FREE guest wi-fi.

This is great for instant messaging, using the My Disney Experience app and general web browsing. It can be patchy at times however and isn't the fastest. I wouldn't rely on it for streaming *Netflix* in your hotel room for example.

9. Don't be afraid to get lost.

Hopefully by now you'll realise that Walt Disney World is big. It's only natural to get lost, especially if you've never been before. However, the cast members at Disney are never far away and will always be able to point you in the right direction (even if it's just finding the nearest restroom).

10. Be camera courteous.

You'll of course want to take pictures and videos during your trip. Whilst doing so, don't forget about the people around you. Try not to bring an iPad to film the fireworks and know ahead of time that selfie-sticks are banned in all Disney parks. It's also courteous to turn your flash off on rides and for fireworks and shows.

11. Security is tight.

Security is big in Disney. There are multiple types of security in use to keep you safe but you'll likely only notice a couple. If you're not naughty, you won't have a problem. Do however give yourself time for security checks at each park.

12. Tipping means something.

If you're from the UK, you're likely used to tipping only when service is beyond exceptional, safe in the knowledge staff are being paid a fair wage. In America, tipping isn't just a gesture, it's a custom. Servers in Walt Disney World for example get paid about $5 an hour (£3.50ish).

Tipping will always be at your discretion. However, I feel it's worth me explaining the tipping culture if you're not already familiar.

Some cast members won't make enough to support their family if a number of guests choose not to tip them that day. Coming from the UK, I appreciate the feeling of being confused by the American culture around tipping. However, it is what it is and having been on the other side of the equation, I know how much particular cast members rely on tips to live and what it means for someone to not tip when they've been provided a service.

A GUIDE TO TIPPING

Large Dining Parties - If you're a party of 8 or more, an 18% gratuity will be added to your bill. Servers normally have 3 or 4 tables. So this policy considers that if the server has a large party taking up most of their section for a hour or two, they cannot be left short for the service they have provided.

Servers and Bar Staff - Cast members in these roles are paid less than others. This is with the consideration that their role is 'tipped.' If buying a drink at a bar, it's customary to tip $1 per prepared drink. If you're dining at a table service restaurant where you're served by a cast member, consider the below percentages for working out how much to tip. If your server is terrible, of course you shouldn't tip them. However, I recommend speaking with a manger to explain why the service was terrible and why you won't be tipping.

JUST OK	GOOD	GREAT
15%	18%	20%+

Minnie Van Drivers - Should you treat yourself to a Minnie Van ride during your stay, you have the option of tipping in cash or via the Lyft app. Depending on the length of the journey I'd typically tip $3-10 depending on the driver.

Bell Services - If you choose to have bell services store your bags, pick them up from your room or drop them off at your room, I recommend tipping the host or hostess that assists you $1 per item of luggage. If I'm leaving my case with bell services on my last day for example, I'll typically tip when I pick them up.

Disney's Magical Express - If you choose to utilise Disney's free airport shuttle service, consider tipping the driver after your journey. Personally I opt for $1-2 per person, per journey. I've never had a bad driver and they're loading and unloading a lot of cases. They don't often expect it either.

Housekeeping - At Walt Disney World, your room should be serviced once a day. As you'll unlikely have the same housekeeper for every day of your holiday, I'd recommend leaving a tip each day, rather than a large tip at the end of your stay. I've opted for tipping $1-2 per day, per person using the room. I've also noticed that the housekeepers I've left tips for, have at times gone a little further to make my room even more magical.

Valet - If you choose to leave your car with the valet at the front of your Disney resort hotel (or at Disney Springs), I believe it's customary to tip when you drop off your car and when you pick it up. I don't have a real experience using this service but if the cast member assisting you has to run in the rain, consider tipping them more than just a couple of dollars.

Un-Tipped Cast Members - Not all cast members are allowed to accept tips. On occasion, a particular cast member may go above and beyond the call of duty. In this instance you may like to tip them as a way of thanks. However, don't be offended if they ask you to keep it. If a cast member is paid a certain hourly rate, they're not allowed to accept tips. However, a cast compliment can be a great way of thanking this cast member (page 105).

13. Disney Skyliner

Easily one of the best additions to Walt Disney World, this new gondola system provides quicker transportation between: Epcot, Hollywood Studios, Disney's Riviera Resort, Disney's Caribbean Beach, Disney's Art of Animation and Disney's Pop Century.

Each cabin can hold up to 10 guests. Guests will board as the gondola moves slowly through the station before it picks up speed when mounting the cable system.

Transferring

Caribbean Beach is the main station for the Skyliner. Within this hub, there are three lines that terminate. Here is where you will transfer to get to various destinations. For example, you'll need to change here if travelling between Epcot and Hollywood Studios.

Delays and Stops

On occasion, the cable will slow or stop. This is perfectly normal and is to allow for cast members to assist a guest with any trouble boarding/disembarking the gondola. This is more typical on the Epcot line as Riviera doesn't have a dedicated special assistance station.

Emergency Procedure

In the event of a personal emergency, call boxes are located within each cabin. Should the system shut down, local authorities are trained to assist in a full system evacuation. Additionally, an emergency kit is located in each cabin which can be opened upon authorisation from a cast member.

Scared of Heights?

From someone who's scared of heights and claustrophobic, I'm pleased to say I love the Skyliner. It's a smooth journey, is beautifully quiet and can actually be very relaxing. If you're nervous and would like to 'try it out', I recommend travelling from Caribbean Beach to Pop Century/Art of Animation.

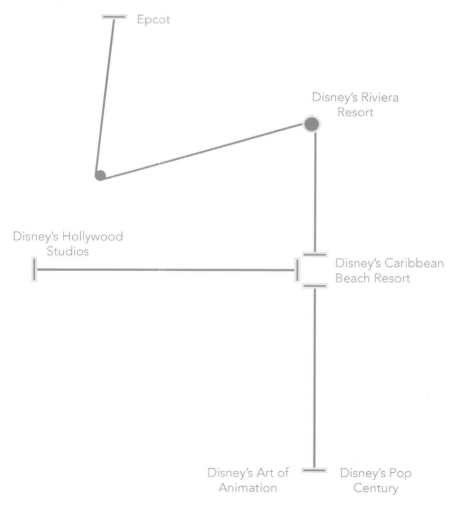

14. It's going to rain... A lot!

It storms a lot in Florida, to the extent that Florida is the world capital for lightening strikes. No matter the time of year you're going, you're most likely going to get a few hours of rain. The only time of year you could potentially go an entire holiday without rain is December - March.

PRO TIP

If rain is forecast, consider taking some flip-flops with you. Change into them when it starts raining to carry on with your day and keep your trainers nice and dry.

If you're travelling in Summer, expect it to rain every day between 3 - 5pm. Here's a couple of handy tips for the managing the rain:

⭐ **Download a Weather Radar App** - The essential app for your time in Florida. Within 20 minutes, a storm can blow into your location. Most weather information is somewhat helpful but a radar will let you see what's heading your way in real-time.

⭐ **Store your Rain Gear** - If you're travelling with a few people, you don't want to be carrying lots of ponchos, flip flops and umbrellas all day. For that reason, consider renting a locker located at the main entrance of each park. This will allow you to drop off all your rain gear when it's clear and sunny. Keep an eye on your weather apps and when there's a storm coming, send one person to go grab the supplies.

* **Prepare for Closures** - If lightening comes within a particular radius of the parks, most outdoor attractions, merchandise and food locations are required to close for safety reasons. During the times where storms are most likely, book fastpasses for indoor attractions or get in line for an indoor attraction when your radar app shows an approaching storm.

* **Bide Your Time** - The first thing that happens when the heavens open is people leave the park. If you've come prepared for the rain, you'll find the park considerably quieter during and after the rain. Not to mention, all those outdoor attractions that have been closed will re-open with no lines! Big Thunder Mountain is a classic example of this. When the rain stops, head to these types of attractions. Just note it takes them about 30 minutes to get the all clear and for the attraction to get up and running again.

15. Alcohol

The minimum drinking age in the state of Florida is 21 years old. If you're from the UK, this may be annoying if you've got people between 18-21 years old with you. However, the drinking age in Florida is very strictly enforced and this is something Disney takes very seriously.

If you're planning on handing off drinks to anyone underage or even trying to buy drinks underage, be prepared to not only get kicked out of the parks but to potentially be arrested.

Acceptable forms of I.D. are a U.S. issued driving license, a Passport or an international government issued I.D. WITH a copy or digital photograph of a passport. So if you're from the UK, just your driving license won't get you served. Either take a photo of your passport on your phone or have a photocopy with you to show alongside your driving license.

16. Photopass

Ever had a holiday where one person is always left out of the photo? Maybe you've been excited to buy an on-ride photo, only to find out they're charging you an arm and a leg? With Photopass, there's options for getting the very best pictures from your trip and saving a great deal of money in the process.

⭐ **Memory Maker** - This is like a dining plan for photos. If not included in your park ticket, you can choose to buy this service ahead of your stay (currently $169 if bought at least 3 days in advance) or when you arrive (currently $199). This allows you to download as many digital photos from your stay as you like. Meaning you'll be able to get all of your on-ride photos, character meet & greet photos and from those with photographers around the park (e.g. photographers stationed in front of Cinderella's castle) at no extra charge.

⭐ **Magic Shots** - With most Photopass photographers, you'll be able get 'magic shots'. These place Disney characters in the photo with you or maybe have you floating away with a bunch of balloons! Just ask your Photopass photographer if they have magic shots available (not all of them do).

⭐ **Zoom Shots** - The latest addition to Photopass is a new type of zoom photo that captures both a wide shot of the landscape and a close-up of your party within that landscape. It then stitches these photos together to offer you a fantastic video memory. These services currently only operate when it's dry/sunny. The most popular zoom shot can be found in Magic Kingdom at the hub. Just head toward the hub grass on the right-hand side as you come in and look for a cast member with a tablet and some masking tape on the pavement to mark the queue.

17. Fastpasses

Disney's FastPass+ system allows you to book reduced wait times for select attractions in each of the four theme parks. It's available to on-site and off-site guests. However, on-site guests get some early booking advantages. To make the most out of FastPass+, visit page 73.

18. Guests with Disabilities

Disney do an amazing job of catering for all guests, no matter who they are or what their disability may be. Disney has a range of services that allow all guests to have an equal or as similar as possible experience. Whilst I suggest calling or visiting guest services to discuss individual needs, here's what I know:

★ **DAS Pass** - Disney provides a service known as Disability Access Service. This enables guests with a disability (including non-apparent) to use an adjusted waiting system when a disability may not allow you to wait in a standing line.

★ **Mobility** - If a guest's disability effects their mobility (e.g. they're required to use a wheel chair most of the time), the majority of lines for attractions are fully accessible (or they offer alternative lines when necessary).

★ **Sight/Hearing** - If a guest is hard of hearing or visually impaired, guests may obtain a handheld device that can offer assistance such as closed captioning and assistive listening. Devices can be obtained at guest relations.

★ **Quiet Spaces** - Sometimes the parks get a bit 'much.' Check out the quiet spaces section for each park, later on in the guide.

19. Allergies

If someone in your party suffers from food allergies, it can be a constant worry that it's going to be difficult eating in restaurants. If you're a parent travelling with a little one with severe allergies, you're likely used to being in control. However, I'm here to assure you, you'll have plenty of options.

Disney has a well established allergy practice at all quick service and table service dining locations. The most important thing however, is for you to **let the first cast member you interact with know, that you have an allergy in your party**. This will in most cases be the restaurant greeter.

For most allergies, it'll be as simple as ordering from an allergy menu. These cater for common allergies such as dairy, eggs, gluten, peanuts etc. It's your responsibility to read this menu and order from it responsibly. You can however ask to speak with a chef if you have any questions.

If an allergy is not listed on these menus or is of high risk, let your server know what allergy you have and that you'd like to speak to a chef. Your server will give the chef a heads-up as to what your allergy is, allowing them to consult any recipes before speaking with you (and helping you order quicker). If requesting to see a chef, try to be patient as they're one of the busiest cast members in each location.

Chefs are specially trained to handle allergies with special attention and will in most cases have seen it all before. Don't be afraid to ask to speak to a chef whenever you have any questions or doubts. Disney takes safety incredibly seriously and is why they have strict allergy processes in-place to keep all guests safe.

20. Strollers (Prams / Push Chairs)

Little one's will often need strollers when at Disney, just because of how much walking they'll be doing. Even kids that haven't used a stroller for a while, may need one at Disney. Here's a couple of tips and tricks I've learnt from my days amongst strollers.

★ Stroller Parking - For safety reasons, strollers cannot be taken into certain spaces. This includes attractions, shows, dining locations or pavilions within the parks. It's with this you'll need to park your stroller in a designated area outside the venue. Ask a cast member if you don't know where it is.

★ Bring a Cover - As your stroller will be outside in stroller parking, it's important to bring a cover to keep it dry in the event of a storm.

★ Size Restrictions - Some people like that a stroller can hold their child, their bag, their merchandise and the kitchen sink. However, guests should note that Disney has implemented size restrictions for strollers. A stroller can be no larger than 31 inches wide and 52 inches long. If you'd like double stroller for your trip, consider one that places one child in-front of the other.

★ Disney Transport - For most methods of Disney Transport, you'll be required to fold your stroller before boarding. This is where a smaller stroller comes in very handy. I can't tell you the amount of times I've seen parents struggling to fold massive strollers, clambering onto the bus and taking up three seats whilst the other parent has to manage the other children.

★ Stroller / Wheelchair Rentals - I speak from experience when I say, sometimes the unexpected happens. Someone twists their ankle or a child you never expected to whine about walking gives up. It's with this you can rent strollers or wheelchairs from the front of each park (for a fee).

21. Meeting Characters

Characters are a huge part of the Disney experience. The best way to find where characters are going to be is on the My Disney Experience app. Here you'll find a handy symbol that labels character locations and times they'll be appearing.

For most characters you'll need to line-up. However, a number of them offer FastPass+ booking and Disability Access Service. Some characters have designated times (like Snow White in Epcot) and their line will be closed when it's coming towards the end of their set. Others will be continuous but don't be alarmed if Pluto leaves to get a bowl of water. He'll be right back.

All characters will be with an attendant. They are there to manage the line and look after the character throughout their set. They'll often be happy to take pictures for you when a photographer isn't around.

When meeting the characters, try to keep the magic alive for the little ones around you. Ask Cinderella about her Fairy Godmother, tell Daisy she's looking fabulous or let Donald know you think he's number one. Some people (I'm not saying you) may choose to test the magic with what they say to characters or ask cast members. Magic is real, especially in Disney. Let's just leave it at that.

Tips for Meeting Characters

⭐ **Be Courteous to Other Guests** - If you're in line and someone ahead of you is currently with a character, don't rush them. This may be the only character they've wanted to meet all holiday. Likewise, if you like to chat with the characters, by all means do; just keep other guests in mind with how long you choose to talk to them.

⭐ **Photographers** - Some photographers will get involved suggesting poses and taking a couple of snaps. However, if you want another picture or specific pose, just ask.

⭐ **Autographs** - Whilst most characters are more than happy to sign autograph books, some may not have opposable thumbs to be able to do so (e.g. Baymax and Olaf). To help characters, I recommend getting clickable sharpies and to open your autograph book to the next blank page.

⭐ **Bags** - When you're next in line, remove your bags. When you go to meet the character, place these down toward the exit to help the cast members.

22. Show Times

Disney has some of the best shows in the theme park industry! With that, you won't want to miss some of them. My advice is to check the Times Guide (either on paper or in the My Disney Experience app) and arrive 15-30 minutes before show time. This is to ensure you get a good view.

Due to limited capacity, some shows may fill up before the show's even close to starting. My advice is to stop-by ahead of the show you'd like to catch and ask a cast member how far in advance they recommend you arrive.

23. Parade & Fireworks

When it comes to one time performances like the parade and fireworks, don't be afraid to get a spot about 45 minutes before the show. Especially with the parade, if you want a spot in the shade - expect to wait for it. This is the process I'd recommend for your first time watching any given performance.

Once you've seen something before, you've got the opportunity to rock-up last minute and try your luck. When it comes to fireworks in Epcot, don't worry too much about getting a spot directly on the lagoon. The World Showcase promenade is so wide, that even back from the lagoon-side you'll have a great view of the fireworks. The only time rocking-up last minute doesn't work, is during busy times with performances that have a limited capacity such as Fantasmic in Hollywood Studios.

24. Smoking Areas

Smoking and vaping is not permitted anywhere inside the theme parks. This is enforced by all cast members for the comfort and well-being of all guests. Designated smoking areas are located outside the theme parks and in select areas at the resorts and at Disney Springs.

PRO TIP

Measure any little ones before departure and review the height requirements on Disney World's website to manage expectations.

25. Height Requirements

Most rides at Disney have a height requirement. If a little one doesn't measure-up, know that there is no amount of bargaining or pleading that'll let them through. It's a restriction for a reason.

26. Merchandise

You're bound to 'treat-yo-self' on your dream holiday. The following tips will help make your shopping time as magical as can be.

- ⭐ **See It, Get It** - If you see something you like, don't assume you'll be able to get it later on your trip. More often than you think, sought-after products will sell out and aren't always stocked elsewhere.
- ⭐ **Resort Delivery** - If you're staying on-property, you can send your merchandise back to the hotel. This will be available for collection from your hotel merchandise store after 4pm the next day. As such, this service cannot be used on your last couple of days.
- ⭐ **Package Pick-Up** - If in a theme park shop, you can send your merchandise to the front of the park for pick-up on the way out! Just know the package pick-up point is very busy at the end of each day.

PRO TIP

At the start of your holiday, make a trip over to Premium Outlets on Vineland Avenue (a ride-share is normally less that $10 each way). There you'll find a magical little store called Disney's Character Warehouse. Within this store you'll find official Disney Parks merchandise that's on sale. This is great for treating little ones to Disney souvenirs, without breaking the bank.

27. Emergencies

For minor injuries, visit First Aid within the parks or ask to see a first aider when outside of the parks. For major injuries or fire, call 911 and tell the operator you're in Walt Disney World and need Reedy Creek. They're Disney's on-site response team. Any other major emergencies, call 911.

28. Room Occupied Policy

Unlike other hotels you may have stayed in, Disney has a room occupied policy, rather than a standard do no disturb sign. The room occupied policy means that whilst you're welcome to turn down housekeeping and use your hotel room for privacy, a Disney cast member is required to enter the room every 24 hours. This is for the improved safety of all guests.

29. Drinking Water

It's so important to stay hydrated during your stay in Florida. It's recommended to drink about eight pints of water a day (on average). With this, know that the Disney parks all provide regular water fountains and you can get a FREE cup of water from any quick service location.

30. Entering the Parks

It's important to note that your park tickets should be linked to your My Disney Experience account. Without this, your MagicBand will not act as your park ticket. Unless you're staying off property and are only buying a one or two day ticket, this is an essential step for being able to quickly enter the parks.

When you enter the parks for the first time, you'll be required to choose a finger that will be associated with your ticket. You will need to scan this finger each time you enter the parks. My advice is to choose a finger on the opposite hand to where you wear your MagicBand. This will mean you can hold your MagicBand to the reader and scan your finger at the same time, making everything that little bit quicker. Children who's fingers may be too small to scan, may require an adult to use theirs. Make sure this is an adult that will always be entering the parks with them.

31. Season Pricing and Gate Tickets

If you're only planning on visiting Disney for one or two days, you may be thinking about buying your tickets at the gate. When doing this, know that Disney price their tickets based on the season. If it's a peak season day (as defined by Disney online), you'll pay about $40 more than a low season day. You can save yourself a lot of time and money by ordering your tickets online before you arrive. Just make sure the seller is a certified seller (e.g. *Undercover Tourist*).

32. Delivery to a Resort Hotel

If you're making a reasonable journey to Walt Disney World, you may want to order some groceries or online shopping to your hotel. It's important to know that the mailing address for resort hotels is different to that displayed on Google. For the correct address, call +1 407 W-DISNEY (+1 407 934 7639).

Add your arrival date to the name on the delivery and make sure you don't order anything more than a week before check-in. If your delivery arrives during your stay, it should be delivered to your hotel room during the day. All resort deliveries come with a small handling fee (currently $6). It takes about 24 hours to go through Disney's sorting office, so count that into your order timings.

33. Annual Pass

Don't think an annual pass is only for those that are going to be visiting all the time! A Walt Disney World annual pass allows you to get 20% off merchandise (excluding select limited edition merchandise), up to 20% off select dining locations, FREE parking at all the parks and even discounts on hotel rooms.

If travelling from the UK, chances are you've got a 14 day or 21 day ticket. The beauty of this ticket, is that it's easy to upgrade one person to an annual pass (approx. $650 to upgrade at the time of publish). If you're likely to plan your next trip within the year, you'll cover that person's admission for next year, save yourself a pretty penny on a room only reservation and get discounts throughout both holidays. If you're travelling with a large party, you could make the money back in just a few trips to the merchandise shops!

If debating whether to get an annual pass for everyone in your travel party, I would only recommend doing so if your likely to visit three or more times within a year period. Otherwise, just stick to one person in your party getting one.

Should you wish to use your passholder discount on a resort stay, just note this is for a room only reservation (so you can't add the dining plan necessarily). Passholder discounts typically become available 3/4 months prior to travel and can only be booked by the state-side call center. To book, call:

+1 407 WDW-STAY
(+1 407 939-7829)

If you'd like to get through to an agent quickly, just keep pressing 0 at the various prompts.

34. Brining in Your Own Food

You're welcome to bring food with you into the parks (as long as it's within reason). For safety reasons, cooler boxes or ice are not allowed into the parks. If looking to keep food cool, consider freezer blocks. Should you wish to bring snacks/lunch into the parks, make sure your food is stored in a transparent box so that you're not held up at security. I strongly advise against using tin foil to wrap your sandwiches as this can spark alarm bells when going through security.

35. Cast Compliments

During your holiday, you may come across a cast member that goes above and beyond to make your trip magical. If you'd like this cast member to be recognised in some way, you can either:

★ Tweet mentioning @WDWGuestService, include the cast member's name, location and how they went above and beyond. You can also use the hashtag #CastCompliment. The cast member's manager will be sent a print out of your tweet and be recognised within their work location.

★ Visit Guest Relations at the entrance of each park or in Town Center at Disney Springs. Here you can send an Applause-o-gram which is a very special recognition. It's not every day a guest will go out of their way to write an Applause-o-gram and it's worth a lot of brownie points to the cast member.

36. Guest Experience Team

Throughout the parks, you may notice cast members dressed in blue under blue umbrellas. These are essentially field guest relations cast members. Whilst they can't do everything, they're able to answer most questions, assist with My Disney Experience, assign DAS pass return times and more.

> **FUN FACT**
>
> More than 70,000 cast members work in Walt Disney World!

37. Minnie Vans

In partnership with Lyft, Disney has created a new transport service to get you around Walt Disney World property and even to/from Orlando International Airport and the Disney Cruise Line Terminal in Port Canaveral.

Firstly, this is a premium service. The price of a Minnie Van ride will often be two or three times the price of a standard Uber or Lyft ride. However, Minnie Vans do come with some advantages that make them well worth the cost on particular journeys.

If travelling to or from Magic Kingdom, Minnie Vans pick-up and drop-off from the Magic Kingdom bus loop. If you were using any other ride-share service, you'd have to get dropped off at the Transportation and Ticket Center, to then get the Monorail or Ferry. This means that utilising a Minnie Van after closing time at Magic Kingdom, will get you back to your resort hotel in no time at all! Minnie Vans can also drop you off right at your resort building. This is unlike other ride-share services that must drop you off at the lobby/check-in area.

To book a Minnie Van for use on Walt Disney World property, you simply use the Lyft app. An active Lyft account is needed to use this app and first-time users can often save a few dollars by checking for offer codes or using a referral code.

My advice is to request your Minnie Van at least 5-10 minutes before you actually need it. Due to a limited number of vehicles across property, you're more likely to be waiting for you Minnie Van than not. For example, if it's closing time at Magic Kingdom, request your Minnie Van as you're walking down Main Street U.S.A toward the exit.

Benefits of a Minnie Van

★ Driven by a Disney cast member. Meaning you're in safe hands and will receive excellent service during your ride.

★ All vehicles carry two high quality child safety seats.

★ Can pick-up/drop-off right at your resort hotel building. Especially helpful when coming back from a long park day.

★ In-car phone chargers.

★ Clean and exceptional standard of vehicle.

★ Disney Parks music from across Walt Disney World property.

Minnie Vans for the Airport or Cruise Terminal

Having tried a Minnie Van from the airport, in my opinion, these journeys are really not worth the money. An airport trip will cost you over $150 and a cruise terminal journey will cost you over $250 each way! However, should you wish to splash out on a special occasion or something, call this number to book:

+1 407 WDW-PLAY (+1 407 939 7529)

Chapter 6
DREAM GUIDE TO MAGIC KINGDOM

Opened in 1971, Magic Kingdom is the single most attended theme park in the world! For me growing up, it was a place of legend and I'd have been so lucky to ever go. Now, I know it like the back of my hand. I've got attraction recommendations, I can let you know where's good to eat and even share how to get a great position for the fireworks.

What I'm not going to do is waste your time here. You've got things to do and characters to see. I'm simply going to share with you my best tips, tricks and advice when it comes to spending a day at Magic Kingdom.

FUN FACT

Cinderella's castle is exactly 189 feet tall. Any taller and Disney would've needed to put a beacon on top to warn aircraft.

TOP TIPS

Whilst I'm going to walk you through as much of the park as I can, there are some top line things everyone should know when visiting Magic Kingdom. These top tips are great if you're on the go and need a little reminder.

★ **Parking** - Magic Kingdom (and all the parks for that matter) require a parking fee. Currently this is $25 per car. When approaching the toll plaza, be ready to pay.

★ **Getting to the park** - The parking lot is HUGE. It'll take some time to walk or use the tram to reach the front of the lot. At the front of the lot is the Transportation and Ticket Center (continue below).

★ **Transportation and Ticket Center (TTC)** - This area is the middle ground between the parking lot and the actual theme park. Between the park and the parking lot is a lake. To get to the park you have to take a monorail or ferry from the TTC. It's in this area you'll go through security and be able to buy tickets if you haven't already (I hope you bought them in advance).

★ **Security** - Since Magic Kingdom is the biggest tourist destination in the world, security is tight! Be prepared to have your bags and strollers checked and go through airport-like security. This is necessary to ensure your safety in the park. It may take some time to get through but Disney has put everything in place for your safety and peace of mind. The security team are always a welcoming face of the park.

★ **Welcome Show** - About 30 minutes before opening time, you'll be able to enter the park and make your way up to Cinderella's castle for the welcome show. When the park officially opens, Mickey and his pals will welcome you to Magic Kingdom with a mini show.

★ **'Rope Drop'**- If you've done some research, you might have seen this term already. It's more literal than it seems. Cast members will block off each land of the Magic Kingdom prior to the official opening with a rope. Once the park has been announced open, guests will be able to explore the rest of the kingdom. Getting to a park for 'rope drop' is just getting there for opening.

★ **Postcards Home** - If you want to send a letter or postcard home, you can send it from Magic Kingdom and have a special stamp added to the envelope. Stamps are sold at the small shop located to the far left of the train station near the entrance.

★ **You'll Need More Than One Day** - With so much to see and do at Magic Kingdom, it's unlikely you'll be able to see everything in just one day.

★ **Rider Swap** - If you've got a little one that's too short for a ride, ask a cast member for a rider swap pass. Only one parent will have to line-up to ride. Once off, swap parenting and the other parent will use the fastpass line.

★ **Shop During the Day** - Some may tell you that because the shops are open late, you should wait until the end of the day to do your shopping. However, the shops are a lot more enjoyable during the day and with delivery services to your hotel or the front of the park, you won't need to carry anything.

Attractions

There are more attractions in Walt Disney World than you can shake a stick at. So whilst I'd love to give you a detailed description of each and every ride, I still want this book to be light enough to take with you on holiday. With that, I'm going to name each attraction, share my priority rating, who I think it's good for (typically speaking) and which weather it's best enjoyed in. If there's a ride you'd like more information for, check the My Disney Experience app or see if there's a video on YouTube that'll give you a point-of-view preview.

PRO TIP

If you've never been to Walt Disney World before, download the My Disney Experience app and browse the park maps as I'm walking you through the parks. You'll get a better idea of what I'm talking about when you see it in-front of you.

Adventureland

Located to the left of Cinderella's castle when entering the park. Adventureland is where I recommend starting your day if you're coming in first thing. Most people turn right when given the choice or head straight to Fantasyland.

Themed like a jungle and featuring the popular Jungle Cruise, you'll feel like you're really on an adventure in this area.

FP

Jungle Cruise

FP

Magic Carpets of Aladdin

FP

Pirates of the Caribbean

Swiss Family Treehouse

Enchanted Tiki Room

FUN FACT

In Pirates of the Caribbean, there are two skeletons stuck playing Chess. If you look at the pieces, you'll notice they're trapped in a stalemate.

Frontierland

Saddle up cowboys and cowgirls, we're headed to the old frontier! With it's western style theming and some of the best attractions in the park, Frontierland is one of my favourite lands to hang out in. Another great land to head to when the park first opens!

PRO TIP

Frontierland is the start of the parade route. Whether you're looking to watch the daytime, Halloween or Christmas parade, it's a little quieter here.

Big Thunder Mountain

It's a roller coaster but one that's all about fun! There's no scary drops or loops, it's just a lot of fun. Possibly my favourite ride in the park or at least my 'must-do.' Big Thunder Mountain is always quietest when the sun goes down and riding it in the dark offers a little extra thrill!

Country Bear Jamboree

Splash Mountain

Tom Sawyer's Island

FUN FACT

Head into Le Chapeau on Main Street U.S.A and find the wall phone. Pick it up and you may just hear the voices of some citizens of Main Street.

PRO TIP

If you're looking for a good place to watch the parade, consider just outside the Christmas Shop courtyard. Perfectly shaded and super close to the fun!

Liberty Square

Think colonial America around the time of the civil war. Here you can see a replica of the Liberty Bell, take a steam boat around Tom Sawyer's Island or venture into the infamous Haunted Mansion. I recommend Momento Mori for some ghostly shopping.

The Hall of Presidents

Haunted Mansion

Liberty Square Riverboat

Fantasyland

Let your inner-child run free in this land of fantasy and make-believe. Featuring some of the most popular and most recognisable Disney attractions, you don't want to miss a lot of these attractions. It's quietest here when the parade is on or during/after the fireworks.

Dumbo the Flying Elephant

Enchanted Tales with Belle

It's A Small World

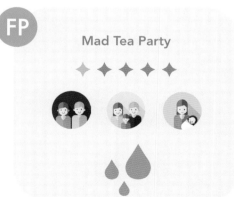

Mad Tea Party

FP Mickey's PhilharMagic

FP Peter Pan's Flight

Prince Charming Regal Carrousel

FP Princess Fairytale Hall

Pete's Silly Sideshow

FP Seven Dwarfs Mine Train

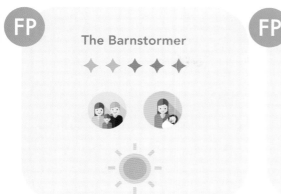

The Barnstormer

The Many Adventures of Winnie The Pooh

Under the Sea: Journey of The Little Mermaid

PRO TIP

Seen the fireworks before and don't want to wait around for a good spot? Consider watching them from the Tangled toilets in Fantasyland.

Tomorrowland

Step into the world of what could've been the future! Styled in a 50s-esque idea of what the future was going to look like, you'll find some of the hottest attractions here. I can easily spend an entire afternoon just hanging about in Tomorrowland.

Buzz Lightyear's Space Ranger Spin

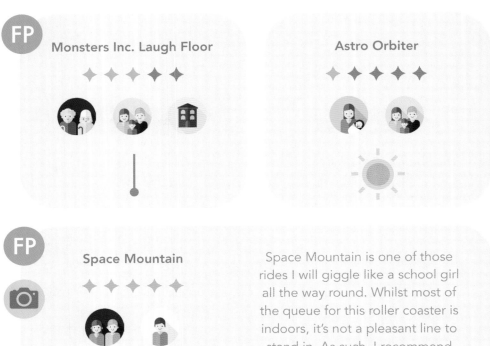

Monsters Inc. Laugh Floor

Astro Orbiter

Space Mountain

Space Mountain is one of those rides I will giggle like a school girl all the way round. Whilst most of the queue for this roller coaster is indoors, it's not a pleasant line to stand in. As such, I recommend using one of your allotted fastpasses for this attraction.

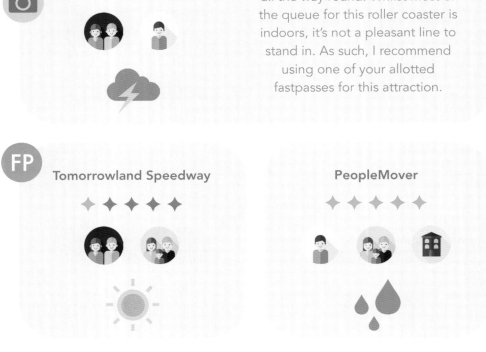

Tomorrowland Speedway

PeopleMover

Carousel of Progress

TRON Lightcycle Power Run

OPENING 2021

Dining

So where does one eat in the most visited theme park on earth? Well, there's more than a few places to grab a snack or sit down for a feast. Having tried every quick service and table service in the park, I'll give you my top recommendations for each style of dining.

Quick Service Dining

The quick service restaurants at Magic Kingdom are busy most of the time. As such, I'd recommend them for families on-the-go.

If possible, try to dine outside of peak meal times for a more relaxing experience. I'd try to avoid: 12pm - 2pm and 5pm - 7pm.

Columbia Harbour House

By far my favourite dining location in Magic Kingdom, this quick service serves New England style home comforts such as Chicken Pot Pie, Lobster Roles and more! Head upstairs for ample seating and a nice chill out from the hustle and bustle of the park.

Be Our Guest

Available at breakfast and lunch, Be Our Guest's quick service is great for Beauty and the Beast fans! How often do you get the chance to dine in the Beast's ballroom? I wouldn't recommend going here for dinner as compared to breakfast and lunch, it's overpriced and not great food.

Pecos Bill Tall Tale Inn & Cafe

If like me, you enjoy Mexican food; you'll likely enjoy grabbing lunch here. With a great selection of what I call 'pick-me-up' food and a free toppings bar, it's well worth your time and money. It can feel a little crowded at times so I wouldn't hang-out here too long.

Table Service Dining

If you're looking for the chance to kick-back, unwind and have a break from a busy day, these table service recommendations may be right for you. I've only included a couple here as there are better table service locations outside of the park.

Skipper Canteen

Whilst the menu may be a little 'out there' for some, the atmosphere and cast member interaction at this location is something truly special! You're served by a Jungle Cruise skipper and they're just as sarcastic and witty as they are out on the Jungle Cruise attraction.

The Crystal Palace

If you're looking for a character breakfast, look no further! Whilst an expensive breakfast, this all-you-care-to-enjoy buffet features Winnie the Pooh and friends, as well as a great selection of food. Reservations are highly recommended for this restaurant.

Quiet Spaces

In Magic Kingdom especially, the parks can feel a little overwhelming. I myself really struggle with crowds. After standing in amongst a lot of people, I just need a little me time to relax before continuing with the day. The below spaces should give you some time to calm down and recuperate.

⭐ **Columbia Harbour House** - The upstairs of this Quick Service dining location, ideally outside of busy dining hours, is quiet and air conditioned.

⭐ **Tom Sawyer's Island** - As long as you don't mind a small boat ride over to the island, this is by far the best place to relax. With rocking chairs and plenty of shade, it's a great place to escape whilst still exploring.

⭐ **Tortuga Tavern** - This quick service is only open when demand requires it to be open. Outside of those times, it's a great place to chill.

⭐ **Hub Grass** - Whilst not that quiet, located in-front of Casey's Corner, you can lay down on astroturf and soak up the sun if you so choose.

⭐ **Tangled Toilets** - Not far from the Haunted Mansion is the Tangled themed area known as the Tangled Toilets. Whilst I'm not suggesting you hang out in the toilets, the space around here is often less busy and a little more relaxing than the rest of the park.

⭐ **First Aid** - Worst comes to worst, head to First Aid if you feel like you may be on the verge of / actually having a panic attack.

Entertainment

Magic Kingdom is entertainment central! With a parade, castle stage show, pop-up shows and more, you'll be spoilt for choice. As Magic Kingdom is targeted at families with young children, the majority of shows will gear more to this audience but will bring a smile to any child at heart.

Mickey's Royal Friendship Faire

Main Street Philharmonic

Dapper Dans

Festival of Fantasy Parade

Rainy Day Cavalcade

If you're lucky enough to be in Magic Kingdom when it's raining (stay with me) and it's not a thunder storm, the Festival of Fantasy parade turns into the Rainy Day Cavalcade. You need a lot of luck to see this parade. If you do, you'll get to see characters in cute rain coats!

Move it! Shake it! Dance & Play it!

Main Street Trolley Show

Happily Ever After (Fireworks)

Here's one for everyone! Happily Ever After is Magic Kingdom's nighttime firework spectacular. This show features projection mapping on the castle, fireworks, lasers and Tinkerbell may even fly through the night (weather permitting).

Merchandise

Everyone loves to treat themselves to a souvenir on holiday! Well, in Magic Kingdom you'll have a lot of choice to satisfy your inner shopaholic. Below are a few tips and tricks to snap up your keepsakes. Don't forget about package pick-up or delivery back to your Walt Disney World hotel.

★ **Main Street Emporium** - By far the largest store in the park, this merchandise location covers all the buildings on the left side of Main Street U.S.A. Whilst it's open about an hour after park closing, I recommend visiting this store about midday. After the parade and after the fireworks are by far the busiest times to shop in here.

★ **Memento Mori** - Located across from Columbia Harbour House is a merchandise store with a twist. This store is dedicated to The Haunted Mansion! Not only can you pick-up some spooky souvenirs, you can also get a haunting portrait done to make you one of the 999 happy haunts.

★ **Art of Disney** - Next door to the Confectionary, this is where you can find some pretty amazing limited edition books, art and collectables.

PRO TIP

If you don't want to wait over an hour for the perfect fireworks view, arrive about 20 minutes before show-time. People sitting on the floor will be asked to stand, which opens-up space. Kindly ask people to excuse you as you make your way to the space at the back of the Walt and Mickey statue. Hasn't failed me yet!

Chapter 7
DREAM GUIDE TO EPCOT

Welcome to my home park!

Epcot is where I proudly represented the United Kingdom for two years within the Rose & Crown pub & restaurant. Having spent my mornings walking to work through the park and countless afternoons enjoying the park, I know this park better than any other.

Opened in 1982, Epcot was the second park to be built in Walt Disney World. Derived from the words experimental, prototype, community of tomorrow - Epcot was originally designed by Walt to be a living and breathing city that had residents experimenting with different ways of living in the modern world.

Whilst Walt's original idea wasn't realised, the park is my personal favourite with state-of-the-art attractions and a showcase of cultures from around the world. Starting back in 2019, Epcot embarked on a new journey to reinvent the look of the park and introduce some outstanding new attractions. As with most refurbishments, Disney will execute each part in phases. With this in mind, excuse the extra pixie dust over the years leading up to 2024.

FUN FACT

Epcot's Spaceship Earth is adorned with 11,324 triangular tiles; the same number of spaces in the parking lot! The gaps in-between the tiles filter rain water into World Showcase lagoon.

TOP TIPS

If you're visiting Epcot, here's some top line tips that will help you navigate your day. As it's a park with a completely different vibe to that of Magic Kingdom, it's best to keep the major differences in mind before visiting.

- ⭐ **Security** - If coming from the bus station, you'll likely see security straight ahead of you (under the monorail station). However, on busy days, Disney will open extra security on the far left side of the monorail station. This side is often quieter and thus quicker.

- ⭐ **Bring ID** - If you'd like to get an alcoholic drink, make sure you have the right ID (page 93).

- ⭐ **International Gateway** - Epcot has the advantage of two entrances. The main entrance is situated in front of Spaceship Earth and the other is nestled in the back between the UK pavilion and the France pavilion on the World Showcase. If you're staying at the Yacht & Beach Club, Boardwalk or Swan & Dolphin hotels, this will be your main entrance to the park. Likewise, this is where the Skyliner station is located, so if you're arriving on the Skyliner, don't be too surprised to find yourself at the back of the park upon entering.

- ⭐ **Tiered FastPass+** - Epcot doesn't have as many attractions to choose from when it comes to fastpasses. This means that the most popular attractions are contained within one tier. You'll only be able to choose one attraction from this tier before selecting your other two from the remaining attractions.

⭐ **Rope Drop** - Hopefully you've read the Magic Kingdom section and know what rope drop is. In Epcot, you'll want to be at the park for opening if you're looking to get on the most rides as possible. As Epcot has a greater attendance past 11am, it's a good idea to get on as many rides as you can in the early hours!

⭐ **World Showcase** - This is the area of the park that features 11 pavilions from around the world. Each pavilion hosts dining and merchandise, with some also including films and attractions. Most of World Showcase doesn't open until 11am and tends to be quieter when it first opens.

⭐ **Lunch on the Showcase** - As I've mentioned above, World Showcase opens at 11am. If you don't have a lunch reservation, head to one of the Showcase restaurants just before 12pm when they open. You'll normally be able to score a walk-in reservation without much of a wait.

⭐ **Harmonious -** Epcot's nighttime show is performed on World Showcase lagoon. You'll want to get a spot about 30 minutes before show time for a great view. However, most of the World Showcase provides ample viewing. I wouldn't recommend Japan, China or Germany however, as these pavilions have islands in front of them that block part of the view.

⭐ **Events** - Epcot is known for it's annual Food & Wine festival (especially amongst locals). This and other festivals however, make the world showcase sometimes uncomfortably busy. If visiting during an event, try and complete the Showcase before 4pm to avoid large crowds and long lines.

Attractions

One of the great things about Epcot is that almost every attraction is undercover. If you're forecast rain on your holiday, see if you can make it to Epcot for this day. When storms hit, there's very little in Epcot that has to close.

Epcot has some of my favourite attractions! Frozen Ever After is a must-do for any Frozen fan and Test Track will satisfy anyone with a need for speed!

World Celebration

As part of Epcot's transformation, the former Future World has been spilt into different sections that better embody the areas themes. World Celebration is now the spine of the park, encompassing the front entrance and the middle walkway up to World Showcase.

World Nature

Celebrating the wonders of our world, the attractions in World Nature focus on how we interact with the natural world. Here you can soar over the Great Wall of China, find yourself in the middle of a giant aquarium or even learn how Walt Disney World grow their own food!

Turtle Talk with Crush

Mission: Space

Test Track

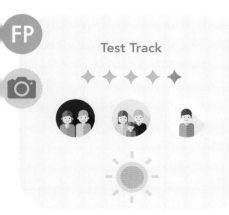

World Discovery

The home of innovative attractions and a step into the future! World Discovery is dedicated to the pioneers and the explorers who are willing to blast into outer space, design and test their own car or even rock out with the Guardians of the Galaxy on a one-of-a-kind coaster.

If you suffer from ANY level of motion sickness, this is not the ride for you. Despite this attraction offering a less and more intense option, neither option is particularly comfortable. If you do choose to ride, I always recommend starting on the green option.

Guardians of the Galaxy: Cosmic Rewind

OPENING 2021

Play Pavilion

OPENING 2021/2022

World Showcase

Focussing on eleven cultures from around the world, Disney has done a great job of adding attractions that enlighten the experience of these cultures. Some feature characters you're familiar with and others are movies that actually show you the country from a moment in time.

Grand Fiesta Tour

Frozen Ever After

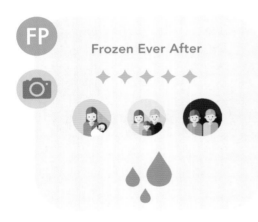

FUN FACT

World Showcase is approximately 1.2 miles in length. As such, comfortable footwear is a must when visiting Epcot.

Wondrous China

American Adventure

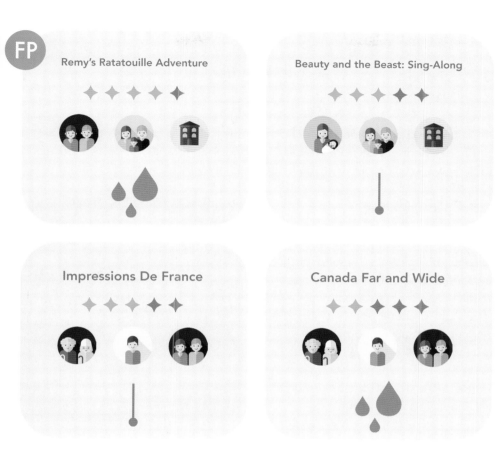

Remy's Ratatouille Adventure

Beauty and the Beast: Sing-Along

Impressions De France

Canada Far and Wide

PRO TIP

Few guests understand that after you've used your three pre-booked fastpasses, you'll then be able to book a new fastpass one at a time for the rest of your day! This is especially helpful in a park like Epcot where the attractions are split up into tiers. Make sure you use up your pre-booked fastpasses as soon as possible. That way, you can possibly score another tier one attraction!

Dining

If you're looking for good eats, Epcot is the place to be! With more than 10 pavilions offering food from around the world, with a variety of quick service and table service dining options, you'll never be far away from good food.

Quick Service Dining

Epcot is the best place for quick service dining that's beyond burgers and fries! At Epcot, you'll find options in each World Showcase pavilion. You could get Chinese, fish & chips, sushi and a burger, all in one park!

A great way to plan your quick service meals is to check out the menus on the MDE app ahead of your arrival.

Katsura Grill

✦ ✦ ✦ ✦ ✦

Quite possibly my favourite quick service in all of Walt Disney World. This off-the-beaten-track location offers beautiful scenery in it's outdoor seating area and air conditioning inside. I love the Chicken Cutlet Curry here, which is basically a Katsu curry.

Sunshine Seasons

Located in The Land pavilion, this extra large location offers multiple menus! If you've got a lot of people to cater for, this one-stop-shop should make everyone happy. It's also a very good place to wait out a storm if you get a table before the heavens open.

Les Halles Boulangerie-Patisserie

Nestled in the France pavilion is a wonderful bakery. Serving everything from delicate pastries, through to warm sandwiches, this is a great place for brunch! This opens before the rest of the showcase, so it's great if you're coming in through International Gateway.

Regal Eagle Smokehouse

Sometimes, you just want a cheeseburger! Regal Eagle offers ample seating and a good half-way spot along the World Showcase. This is a great spot to kick-back, enjoy some air conditioning and get a great burger! If you're looking for a meaty meal, you'll find it here.

Table Service Dining

Similar to that of quick service offerings, the table service options at Epcot are all something different. You'll be able to find at least one table service location that's just right for you. Reservations are less often a necessity in Epcot but are always recommended.

Tepan Edo

This is the place to be if you're looking for dinner and a show! At Tepan Edo, Japanese chefs will cook your food in front of you whilst also entertaining you along the way. As groups are seated together, it's a nice place to meet other guests if you're flying solo.

Via Napoli Ristorante Pizzeria

Families, look no further than the Italy pavilion for one of the best meals of your holiday. I love my pizza and Via Napoli hasn't disappointed me yet! It offers giant pizzas fit for the whole family and a wonderful design. This is somewhere you should book ahead!

Garden Grill

Garden Grill is an all-you-care-to-enjoy character dining experience. Not only that, the restaurant is on a slow moving turn-table located in the middle of The Land. Not only does the Thanksgiving style meal come to your table, you get an ever changing view from your table.

Biergarten Restaurant

This restaurant works a little different to most. Regardless of party size, you will be sat on a long table of 10. If you've got a big family, then this is perfect. The buffet isn't to everyone's taste (as it's quiet heavy food) but the atmosphere and show are great!

FUN FACT

At The Rose and Crown in the UK Pavilion, you may notice some oddly shaped glass windows that distort the view inside. These harken back to a time that most British pubs used these windows to offer a level of security to their patrons. If their wives came looking for them, they couldn't see whether their husband was definitely inside or not.

Quiet Spaces

Epcot isn't too bad when it comes to crowds. Thanks to the large open spaces and the promenade being so wide around the World Showcase, it's pretty easy to find some rest spots. However, there may come a time that the crowds are just a little too much (e.g. during festival season or American holidays). The following locations will allow you to gather yourself in a quiet and cool space.

⭐ **Canada Theatre** - Just before going into the Canada Far and Wide theatre, there's a large air conditioned waiting room. If a show's just started, this becomes a wonderfully quiet room to chill in.

⭐ **Japan Pavilion Gallery** - Located next to the amazing Mitsukoshi store.

⭐ **Morocco Pavilion Museum** - Behind an inconspicuous door at the front of the pavilion (on the left). It took me four years to find this place! It's probably the best place to recover from a busy/hot day. Because of it's disguised entrance, very few guests dare open the doors. There's a couple of benches inside too.

⭐ **Norwegian Church** - Similar to the museum in Morocco, few people know you can go inside the wooden church in Norway. Making it a lovely little quiet space to just calm down. This room doesn't have any seating however and has a little more footfall than Morocco's museum.

⭐ **First Aid** - Worst comes to worst, head to First Aid if you feel like you may be on the verge of / actually having a panic attack.

Entertainment

As part of Epcot's transformation, entertainment offerings are currently being reviewed and updated. With this in mind, keep an eye out for new offerings coming soon and know that some of the following entertainment is likely to change from the time of this book going to print.

Jewelled Dragon Acrobats (China)

Mariachi Cobre (Mexico)

Voices of Liberty (America)

Harmonious (Fireworks)

Each evening, World Showcase Lagoon is brought to life with state-of-the-art lighting, pyrotechnics and music, the perfect end to your day in Epcot.

Merchandise

If you're looking for shopping with a difference, you'll find a variety of international and Disney merchandise at Epcot. Below are a few recommendations if you're looking to pick-up some special souvenirs.

⭐ **Mouse Gear** - The main store in Epcot, Mouse Gear is your one-stop-shop if you're looking to give the little one's their pocket money and let them go wild. Mouse Gear is also pretty good for having stock when other stores on property have run out (thanks to it's large stock room). If there's a limited edition item you're having a hard time finding, pop into Mouse Gear and ask a cast member if they can check for you.

⭐ **Mitsukoshi** - Located in the Japan pavilion, this large store celebrates the fandoms popular in Japan and culture of the country. If you like Pokémon, Hello Kitty or you'd like to try some Japanese candy, this is the store for you. There's also a fun pearl experience that allows you to pick a clam from a tank and have a small demonstration performed by the Japanese cast members.

⭐ **German Pavilion** - I might be cheating by saying all of the shops in the German Pavilion but it's my favourite pavilion! I highly recommend checking out their cuckoo clocks, the Christmas decorations shop and I cannot recommend the Werther's confectionery enough (please try the chocolate covered strawberry).

FUN FACT

In creating the Morocco pavilion, the king of Morocco sent over his personal architect to work with Disney Imagineers to get the design of the pavilion just right.

Festivals

Throughout the year, Epcot is transformed for a variety of seasonal festivals. From mid January is the Festival of the Arts, the Flower and Garden Festival is from March until early summer, the International Food and Wine Festival kicks off in late summer, which is closely followed by Festival of the Holidays from November until the New Year.

Whilst each of these festivals are very different, there are some essential tips that apply to most, if not all of them.

★ **Snack Credits** - If you've got a Disney Dining Plan as part of your trip, consider spending most of your snack credits on the festival food stalls! These are often a great use of snack credit. Whilst a snack credit typically covers something around the $5 mark, you could easily get a small dish worth $8 for one snack credit! Every credit counts when you're on a dining plan!

★ **Go Early** - Locals love the festivals. They'll typically come to Epcot after 4pm. As such, World Showcase gets very busy after this time. If you're travelling with young children, I recommend completing the festival before this time. Just as some guests may become more and more inebriated.

★ **Sampling Packages** - These will often allow you to try a few glasses of alcohol in different locations and save a little money compared to buying them separately. Look out for the offers posted at the registers.

Chapter 8
DREAM GUIDE TO HOLLYWOOD STUDIOS

Disney's Hollywood Studios is the home of the movies! Opened in 1989 as Disney MGM Studios, the park was originally designed to put you behind-the-scenes of the movies. However, the park is now designed around the idea of placing you inside the movies. With the likes of Star Wars: Galaxy's Edge, Toy Story Land and Mickey and Minnie's Runaway Railway, the park has a new lease of life which has made this one of the busiest parks day-to-day.

Included in this Dream Guide to Hollywood Studios, is also a Dream Guide to Star Wars: Galaxy's Edge. Here I'll explain some of the things that make this part of the park completely different to anything you've seen before. Turn to page 148 if you're looking to make the most of your visit to Galaxy's Edge.

TOP TIPS

With so many new additions to the park in recent years, you may be unfamiliar with how this park may have changed since your last visit. The following tips are designed to cover the basics of Hollywood Studios for visitors new and returning.

- ⭐ **Tiered FastPass+** - Like Epcot, a select number of attractions are kept within a top tier. In order to best utilise your fastpasses, consider which of the top tier attractions is highest on your list of priorities. For the other top tier attractions, consider booking these for an alternative day or getting in line at the very end of the day. Don't forget to try for more fastpasses once you've used up your three.

- ⭐ **Save the Shows** - If you arrive at Hollywood Studios in good time, avoid seeing any of the shows in the morning/early afternoon. The shows are a great way to cool down later in the day and rest-up. Likewise, the first few showings are normally the busiest.

- ⭐ **Fantasmic** - This is Hollywood Studios' nighttime show. Great for those that love classic Disney characters and the villains especially. The only problem with Fantasmic is that it has a limited seating capacity. This means that on busy days, you'll be pressed to get a decent view of the show if you turn up anything less than 45 minutes prior to show time. If you can, book a fastpass for the show after you've used up your initial three. There tends to be availability right up until show-time most days.

⭐ **Dining Reservations** - Hollywood Studios is more limited in its table service dining compared to other parks. Not only are their fewer restaurants for the number of daily guests, they're a lot smaller in capacity. As such, I strongly recommend making reservations if you'd like to dine at a restaurant.

⭐ **Mornings** - With so many new attractions to enjoy, the park is incredibly popular first thing in the morning. If you're looking to line up for popular attractions like Slinky Dog Dash, Rock 'N' Roller Coaster, Millennium Falcon etc. Consider visiting after 5pm. The park gets quieter as the day goes on and lines are incredibly short just before closing time (as other guests prioritise the nighttime shows).

⭐ **Fireworks -** If choosing to stick around for the fireworks in the evening, note that the main firing pad is off to the right of the Chinese Theatre facade. This means, if you're standing too far back on Hollywood Boulevard, you'll miss a large portion of the fireworks. For the best view, stand in the main plaza ahead of the Keystone Clothiers store.

Attractions

From state-of-the-art immersion to fun for the whole family, Hollywood Studios boasts a wide variety of attractions, meaning there's something for everyone here. As a number of these attractions are recent additions to the park, expect longer wait times than you might find at other parks. This is also in part to the fact that Hollywood Studios is the smallest park.

FUN FACT

Beauty and the Beast: Live on Stage debuted at Hollywood Studios on the same day as the feature animation, November 22nd 1991. It's been performing at the park ever since, making it one of the longest running shows on Walt Disney World property.

Mickey & Minnie's Runaway Railway

Located in the former location of the Great Movie Ride, this state-of-the-art attraction places the whole family right into a Mickey Mouse cartoon! It's a whole lot of fun and a must do for any Disney fan!

FP Star Wars:
Rise of Resistance

FP Millennium Falcon:
Smugglers Run

FP Slinky Dog Dash

FP Alien Swirling Saucers

FP Toy Story Midway Mania

FUN FACT

Mickey and Minnie's
Runaway Railway boasts
more hidden Mickey's than
any other attraction! My
favourite appears in the
mirror in Daisy's studio.

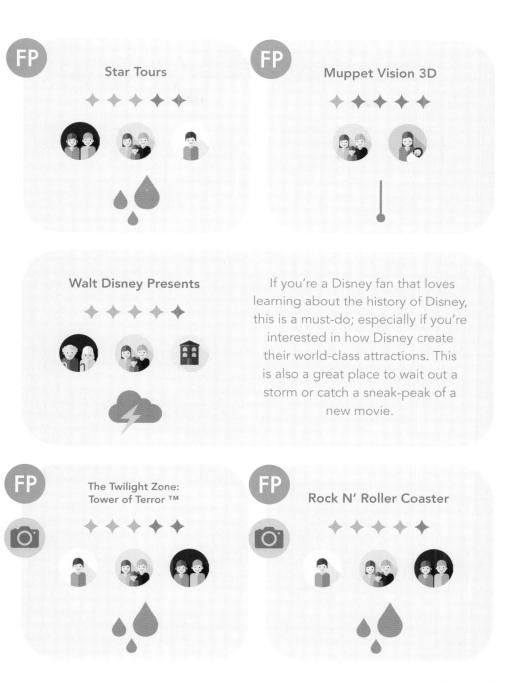

Star Tours

Muppet Vision 3D

Walt Disney Presents

If you're a Disney fan that loves learning about the history of Disney, this is a must-do; especially if you're interested in how Disney create their world-class attractions. This is also a great place to wait out a storm or catch a sneak-peak of a new movie.

The Twilight Zone: Tower of Terror ™

Rock N' Roller Coaster

Star Wars: Galaxy's Edge

Otherwise known as Star Wars Land, Galaxy's Edge marks a big step in immersive entertainment. The land has a level of detail that exceeds that of any other theme park in the world. All of your senses will be telling you you're not on planet earth anymore. There are some things you should know however before you embark on your journey to the planet of Batuu.

For example, the cast members within Galaxy's Edge do not acknowledge they're in a theme park. They're all residents of Black Spire Outpost, on the planet of Batuu. They each have their own back story, unique costume and even use a new language! This guide will make sure you're fully prepared for your adventure, ensuring you get the most out of your time in the land. May the force be with you travellers!

FUN FACT

Galaxy's Edge covers approximately 14 acres. Making it the biggest single themed land expansion to any Disney park.

Rise of Resistance

As the headline attraction of Galaxy's Edge, it's not always easy to get on Rise of Resistance. If however you manage to get on, you're in for one heck of an adventure! By far the most immersive attraction I've ever ridden, you'll feel like you've landed right in the middle of a Star Wars movie on this attraction.

The attraction uses a number of different ride systems and state-of-the-art effects to create a one-of-a-kind experience. If you're unsure whether this experience is right for you, here's an overview of the systems that are used.

You'll move through about five rooms before boarding a ride vehicle. Your ride vehicle works on a trackless system that is very smooth and can move in all directions over the floor.

Within the attraction, your vehicle will make one sudden climb in a lift system, make sudden turns and board a mild simulator that features a short sudden drop.

This attraction may be frightening to some young children but I'd recommend it for most guests. Consult the information board provided at the entrance to the attraction to see whether any elements of the ride may be unsuitable for anyone in your party.

Millennium Falcon: Smugglers Run

If you've ever dreamed of flying the Millennium Falcon, then this is your chance! This is a motion simulator type system but it's not as intense as Mission: Space or Star Tours in my opinion.

Each cabin seats six guests. Within the cabin, there are three positions: pilot, gunner and engineer. These positions are assigned just after the pre-show featuring Hondo Ohnaka and Chewbacca. If you'd like to request a particular position, ask the cast member handing out cards at the end of the jetway. You'll have between 30 seconds and 3 minutes to look around the Falcon's lounge before being called for boarding.

Engineer is my favourite position. This is seated at the back of the cabin, meaning you get to see the whole experience. I'd say gunner is the least labour intensive, so if you're looking to get some pictures of your family in the pilot role, sit here. If you're a pilot, the right-hand pilot has the advantage of the light speed control.

The Phrases of Batuu

Whilst visiting Galaxy's Edge, you'll often hear phrases as you interact with cast members. Most guests are a little thrown off initially, especially when asking where the restrooms are for example and the cast member replies with "the refresher is over there." The following decoder however means you'll have an idea of what-on-earth they're saying before you've arrived. Most guests will pick it up as they go and join in to be part of the story.

Batuu Phrase	English
Bright Suns	Hello / Good Morning
Rising Moons	Good Evening
On Planet	Within Galaxy's Edge
Off World	Outside Galaxy's Edge
Refresher	Restroom / Bathroom
Hydrator	Water Fountain
Ignite the Spark	Resistance Greeting
Light the Fire	Callback to 'Ignite the Spark'
For the Order	First Order Greeting
Cargo Slip	Receipt
Datapad	Mobile Phone
Credits	Amount in Dollars
Scan	Photo / Picture
Travellers	Visitors to Batuu
Younglings / Padawans	Children
Only the Ancients Know	I Don't Know
Til the Spire	Goodbye

Food & Drink

A big part of the immersion, is the unique snack, quick-service and drink options available around the land. Some of the options are better than others however, so I'll hopefully save you from wasting your precious credits on something too out-of-this-world for most.

- Milk Stand

Here you'll have a choice of trying the infamous blue or green milk. If you were asking me which is better, I'd recommend the blue over the green. Truth be told, neither are particularly breathtaking. It's a pricey small drink that doesn't really taste what you'd expect it to. Blue milk is more like a drinkable blueberry Dole-whip, whilst green milk is more similar to children's medicine in my opinion.

- Kat Saka's Kettle

Two different types of popcorn are available here. The green is more similar to a butter/salted combo. The red and purple is a sweet and spicy option. If you're looking for the safe option, stick with the green.

You can also get a souvenir popcorn bucket from here in the shape of a repair droid.

- Oga's Cantina

Perhaps even harder to get into than Rise of Resistance, Oga's Cantina is a lounge and bar. Drinks here are very pricey. However, the atmosphere is something special if you're able to get a reservation. If you're looking to wait for entry, I recommend going first thing in the morning or last thing at night.

You'll have the option of standing bar space or a seated option. I would recommend the bar option as it's not the kind of venue you'd choose to hang out in for ages and by sitting at a table, you miss some of the atmosphere that encompasses the bar and room.

- Coca Cola Bottles

Throughout Galaxy's Edge you'll be able to get special Star Wars themed Coca Cola bottles. These are a great souvenir of your time on Batuu. Just be careful when holding them as the top is easily detached. As such, hold them from the bottom to avoid dropping them.

- Ronto Roasters

By far my favourite food item in Galaxy's Edge is the Morning Ronto Wrap. The regular Ronto Wrap is also very good but the breakfast version is something really special if you make it to the park in time.

- Docking Bay 7

This is the quick-service restaurant for the land. The menu is pretty varied with the Endorian Fried Chicken Tip Yip being my personal favourite of the entrées. These meals are a little pricer than other quick-service locations so this could be a good use of a dining plan credit. This location is probably most comparable to Satu'li Canteen in Animal Kingdom.

Characters

Throughout Galaxy's Edge you'll see characters roaming and interacting with guests. It's important to note however that these characters act very differently than elsewhere in Walt Disney World. Rather than being a photo-op for guests, these characters are part of the story and will act as though they're on a mission. With this in mind, they won't be able to pose for pictures.

Merchandise

Throughout Batuu you'll find a variety of themed merchandise locations. These are designed to look like authentic alien planet stores. As such, you won't find any Darth Vader mugs or Star Wars branded t-shirts here. If you're looking for collectables, pop into Dok-Ondar's Den of Antiquities. By far the most interesting of the stores and great for a few easter eggs if you know Star Wars well. If you're looking for cuddly toys, souvenirs, clothing items and Black Spire Outpost branded merchandise, visit the small shops in the The Market Merchants area located next to Ronto Roasters.

Savi's Workshop

Ideal for the biggest Star Wars fan in your family, you can enjoy a 10 minute building experience and come away with your own lightsaber! Priced at approximately $200 per builder, it's not cheap. It is however worth the price in my opinion.

The price includes a pin based on the building set you choose, a high quality metal lightsaber, carry-case and the building show/experience. One person may accompany each builder. Reservations for this experience can be made via My Disney Experience 180 days in advance. Just note your lightsaber won't fit in any standard sized cases and will need to be carried as hand-luggage on any flights.

Droid Depot

As well as some ready-made droids and toys, Droid Depot is where you can build your own remote control droid. Similar to the build a lightsaber experience, reservations can be made 180 days in advance and are highly recommend as the stand-by line moves very slowly.

This experience is priced at approximately $100 per droid. Whilst cheaper than the build a lightsaber experience, I don't think it's as good value. The building area is normally very crowded and loud. Not to mention your droid will take up a lot of valuable luggage space on your way home.

Dining

Out of all the parks, Hollywood Studios is probably the most 'American' when it comes to food. Just like the other parks, the food is part of the theming. If you love a good burger or even American home cooking, this is where to be.

Quick Service Dining

As there's a limited number of table service locations and they're each pretty small, the quick service locations tend to be the best bet for most families at Hollywood Studios.

With that in mind, if there's a day you can dine outside of the busy meal periods, this is the day to do it. Lunch is especially busy at quick service restaurants.

Backlot Express

If like me, you enjoy Disney french fries and chicken nuggets, this is the place for you. With a refillable drinks machine and large selection of indoor seating, it's a great place to take a load off. If there's a storm coming, this isn't a bad place to grab a bite and wait it out.

ABC Commissary

If you're a fan of ABC shows, pop into this quick service for at least a look around. Every so often you'll find props and costumes from some of your favourite ABC TV shows. Seating here can get a little limited when it's lunch time. Outside of this time, it's a great place to cool down.

Sunset Ranch Market

If you're looking for a pick-me-up or you've got a lot of people to feed that all want something different, make your way to Sunset Ranch Market. With multiple snack and lunch options, it's a great place to please everyone. Just note all the seating is outdoors.

Table Service Dining

The great thing about the table service options here, is that they're all a little different. As I mentioned earlier, due to the size of the restaurants and how few there are, it's not always easy to get in for lunch or dinner without a reservation. For that reason, be sure to book ahead.

50's Prime Time Cafe

Here you'll be served by your 'cousin' for the duration of the meal. The cast here are incredible and offer you a unique experience in that if you don't finish your vegetables, you could be in a world of trouble. Even with a reservation, be prepared to wait for your table.

Sci-Fi Dine-In

This restaurant is something right out of a 50's movie! Designed like a drive-in movie theatre, you'll dine in cars! I wouldn't recommend this restaurant if you have an odd number of guests (someone may be sat by themselves) or a large party (as there's limited large tables).

Mama Melrose's

Now one of my favourite theme park restaurants, Mama Melrose's has a very nice family feel about it. Fantastic American-Italian food served in a warm environment that I'd definitely recommend for large families. Additionally, the restaurant is a nice break from the busy park.

Entertainment

If you like a show, you're going to love Hollywood Studios! Boasting more than eight entertainment experiences, you'll have plenty of choice when it comes to a little bit of show-time.

Indiana Jones ™ Epic Stunt Spectacular

For the First Time in Forever: A Frozen Sing-Along Celebration

FP

Voyage of the Little Mermaid

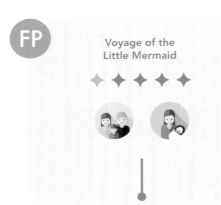

FP

Disney Junior Dance Party

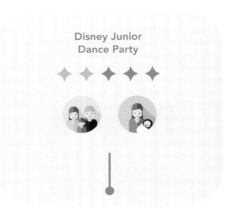

FP

Beauty and the Beast: Live on Stage

FUN FACT

The majority of Fantasmic is run by an automated system and only needs one button to start the whole show.

FP

Fantasmic

Whilst the show's in need of some TLC, it reaches capacity pretty much every evening. As such, I recommend arriving 60-45 minutes prior to showtime. Even with a fastpass, a great view isn't guaranteed. For a guaranteed great view, consider a Fantasmic dining package.

Quiet Spaces

Quiet spaces are a little harder to come-by in Hollywood Studios, especially if you're looking for a sit-down out of the heat. However, here are a few little sweet spots that can get you out of the hustle and bustle and into some air conditioning.

★ **Walt Disney Presents** - Possibly the best place in the park to take a quiet 15, with gentle Disney music playing in the background, it's a lovely place to have a little browse and then there's a screening you can enjoy before re-entering into the park.

★ **Stage 1 Company Store** - Located in the Grand Avenue area, providing there's not a Muppets Vision 3D show letting out, it's a good spot to stop.

★ **ABC Commissary** - Outside of main dining times, this quick service restaurant is both air-conditioned, spacious and quiet.

★ **First Aid** - Located at the front of the park, the first aid center will be able to assist if everything gets a bit 'much' for anyone.

★ **Star Wars Launch Bay** - Located on the opposite side of the park from Galaxy's Edge, this is the meet & greet location for popular Star Wars characters. However, the venue offers lots of space to chill out in and plenty of Star Wars memorabilia/props if you're looking to geek-out whilst you take some time to gather yourself.

★ **Pizza Rizzo** - Whilst only open during peak seasons, this quick service restaurant offers a spacious upstairs dining room that's far quieter than other dining locations in the park.

Chapter 9
DREAM GUIDE TO ANIMAL KINGDOM

If you're looking for a real-life escape from reality, look no further than Animal Kingdom! There are few places that I genuinely forget where I am, even if just for a moment.

Here, theming, dining, music and animals will allow you to disappear into different places around the world and other worlds entirely.

Whilst Animal Kingdom never fails to feel like the hottest place on the planet, it's also the park I'm often most excited to get back to. The amount of detail and accuracy Imagineers put into this park is visible at every turn.

It isn't simply a zoo... It's a place where creative storytelling explores the beauty of animals alongside world-class attractions and shows. Whether it's a show celebrating the animals featured in the Lion King or a trail that leads you into the habitat of gorillas, Animal Kingdom has some adventures for everyone. Not to mention, the incredibly popular Pandora: The World of Avatar.

FUN FACT

In order to create the Tree of Life at Animal Kingdom, imagineers used the basic structure of an off-shore oil rig to make it strong enough to withstand a hurricane.

TOP TIPS

The park's unique design is all meant to evoke exploration and adventure! Whilst it may be a little puzzling to navigate on your first visit, you'll find some tips below that will help any visitor prepare for their day at Animal Kingdom.

★ **Heat & Humidity** - Because of where the park is built, when it's hot, it feels even hotter here. Not only that, the park is packed with trees and foliage. Whilst beautiful, they have a nasty habit of trapping the heat and humidity. With this, be sure to wear light and breathable clothing and make time for regular rest within air conditioned locations. Spray deodorant is also a nice instant cooler on hot days.

★ **Pandora: The World of Avatar** - Opened in 2017, this land remains one of the biggest draws across the whole of Walt Disney World. It's a good idea to know ahead of time that this area of the park is extremely busy from opening until close. If you're without fastpasses for either attraction within the land, I recommend getting in line as soon as the park opens or when the park is about to close.

★ **Tiered FastPass+** - A select number of attractions are kept in a certain tier that'll only allow you to book one of them ahead of time. At the moment, these attractions are Na'vi River Journey and Avatar: Flight of Passage due to their popularity. If Avatar: Flight of Passage is available, it's the one to book when you consider wait times average 2 hours daily.

★ **Animal Activity** - If you're planning to see some animals whilst at Animal Kingdom (which I hope you are) then get to the park as early as possible. If you choose to take a walk along the trails or ride Kilimanjaro Safaris in the morning, you're much more likely to see the animals up and about. Two factors add into this, it's cooler and they've only recently been fed.

★ **Flash Pictures** - When visiting Animal Kingdom, take the courtesy of switching off your flash for the day. Without thinking, you'll be snapping away and may forget the discomfort your camera's flash may have on the animals. This also applies to other guests on Na'vi River Journey.

★ **Nighttime** - Since Disney unveiled Rivers of Light, evenings at Animal Kingdom have gone from quiet to quieter in regard to attractions! After the sun's gone down, head for attractions like Dinosaur, Expedition Everest and those in Dinoland U.S.A. I warn you now however, Expedition Everest at night is not for the faint hearted. I'm not sure how the dark makes it so much more thrilling but I love it!

★ **Rivers of Light** - This is Animal Kingdom's nighttime show. Unless it's a busy time of year, it's unlikely you'll need a fastpass for this show. Whilst beautiful, it doesn't have the same popularity as the other shows across property. This is in part due to the limitations of pyrotechnics around the animals.

★ **Strollers & ECVs** - If there's a park you'd like to try not using a stroller or ECV, I strongly recommend Animal Kingdom for this. With uneven paths and thin promenades, even quiet days can seem a little congested. At busy times, navigating the park without either is still difficult.

Attractions

Since Pandora: The World of Avatar opened at Animal Kingdom, it's now ranked for me as one of the best places for rides! Whilst it's got some great shows, the rides here are each something truly special.

Whilst you won't be spoilt for choice, almost every attraction has something unique over other attractions you may have been on. Where else in the world can you fly on the back of a fictional alien beast?

PRO TIP

Pack your rain gear for Animal Kingdom! There are few attractions that offer escape from the rain when the heavens open. If you come prepared, you'll be able to continue enjoying your day.

Discovery Island

Home of the world famous Tree of Life that towers over the park, Discovery Island is just beyond your welcome to the park.

From Discovery Island you'll be able to venture into the various lands that make up Disney's Animal Kingdom.

It's Tough to be a Bug!

Discovery Island Trails

Pandora: The World of Avatar

By far the most popular land of Animal Kingdom, it's rarely quiet here! With two of the best rides across all of Walt Disney World and some of the best theming seen in the theme park industry, even just walking through this land is an attraction in itself.

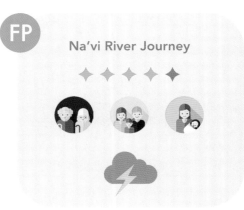

Na'vi River Journey

Avatar: Flight of Passage

Africa

Inspired by the architecture, music and nature of Africa, this is my favourite area of the park for themeing. Especially at night, the Africa land has a certain air about it with the unique lighting and subtle music. Look out for the live musicians during the day!

Gorilla Falls Exploration Trail — FP

Kilimanjaro Safaris

PRO TIP

If you can, ride Kilimanjaro Safaris during or just after rain, you may catch the rare sight of the Elephants playing in the water! I've only been lucky enough to experience this twice but it's worth a shot! A good time to avoid would be any time around or after dusk. Most animals are taken indoors at nightfall which makes the safari far less impressive than during the day.

Asia

Asian food, attractions and animals await in this detailed area of the park. From the jungle through to the Himalayan mountains, this land is incredibly detailed and offers you plenty of exploration opportunities.

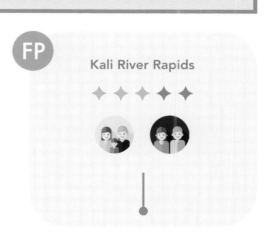

FP

Kali River Rapids

Expedition Everest

Maharajah Jungle Trek

Dinoland U.S.A

Travel back in time to the age of the dinosaurs! Certainly the more kid-friendly area of the park, this land features fantastic character meet and greets, play grounds and a fun fair style theme if you're looking to try your luck on some carnival games.

DINOSAUR

The Boneyard

PRO TIP

If you've got little ones with you, I wouldn't recommend taking them on DINOSAUR if they're frightened of the dark, loud noises or monsters.

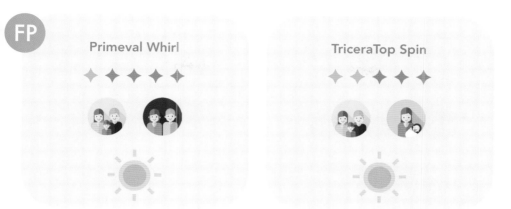

Primeval Whirl

TriceraTop Spin

Dining

Whilst Animal Kingdom is the largest park, a lot of that space is occupied by animals and attractions. Whilst big, it doesn't have as much choice as Magic Kingdom and Epcot.

Quick Service Dining

As I mentioned earlier, Animal Kingdom tends to feel the hottest. Part of that is due to the few locations that actually offer indoor seating and air-conditioning.

That being said, Animal Kingdom has a couple of quick service locations that whilst outdoors, offer some the best affordable in-park food! These locations are popular so plan ahead.

Satu'li Canteen

Offering a selection of bowl dishes in which you can choose your base, meat and topping, this is a quick-service restaurant with a difference. Not only is the food pretty good, the ceiling boasts beautiful hand woven art of Na'vi artwork which add a unique beauty to the location.

Harambe Market

If you're looking for choice and food with a bit of culture mixed in, look no further than Harambe Market! With multiple choices and plenty of seating, it's a popular spot to grab lunch. However, shade can be hard to come-by, so I wouldn't go here if it's too hot.

Yak & Yeti

If you're a fan of Chinese food, make your way to the Yak & Yeti quick service location. My personal favourite here is the honey chicken dish. If you've got a gap to fill but don't want a full meal, the chicken fried rice does a good job of filling that void.

Table Service Dining

There are far fewer table service dining options in Animal Kingdom than other parks. That being said, it's quality over quantity here!

The following restaurants are very different and cater to very different clientele.

Tiffins

This is my favourite table service restaurant! By far the best food I've had in Disney and truly outstanding service. The interior design also encompasses hundreds of pieces of art collected by Imagineers whilst they conducted research for the development of Animal Kingdom.

Tusker House

Whilst I didn't like my dining experience at Tusker House, it's a favourite of many. This is a character dining buffet and whilst I found it a little too loud and close for my liking, I'm aware families love it. I'd recommend going for breakfast based on the feedback I've heard.

Entertainment

Whilst shows aren't in their plenty at Animal Kingdom, you'll be able to find a variety of small pop-up performances around the park. When it comes to night falling over the park, stop by the Tree of Life for 15 minutes or so on your way out of the park. You'll have the chance to see the Tree of Life awaken in the night with beautiful lights, music and projections.

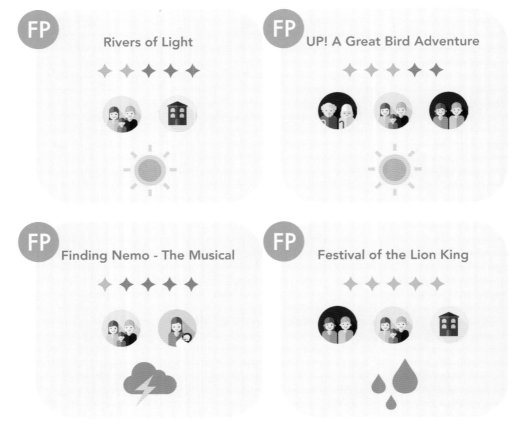

Merchandise

Shopping at Animal Kingdom is a little different from the other parks. Whilst you'll find the main souvenir stores at the front of the park on Discovery Island, a lot of the shopping opportunities are spaced out in small locations. You're more likely to find something special in the smaller locations. For example, Serka Zong Bazaar at the exit of Expedition Everest has some great treasures.

Animals

Throughout the park, you'll find a variety of Animal enclosures. Disney has done a great job of weaving the animals in and around the park to really bring the park to life. However, there's been a careful consideration as to where the animals are placed within the park to ensure they're not disrupted by a roller coaster whizzing by every 60 seconds.

Quiet Spaces

With the heat at Animal Kingdom and thinner than normal paths, it's a good idea to take a little break when you can.

- ★ **Tamu Tamu** - This small quick service location in Africa has some lovely shaded seating which is quiet outside of meal times.

- ★ **Nomad Lounge** - Next door to Tiffins, this is your go-to relaxing space. Whilst you may have to get a drink, it's a comfortable lounge to chill in.

- ★ **Rivers of Light Theatre** - During the day, the theatre around Discovery River opens as a relaxing picnic area. You'll find plenty of space to take a load off, just know there's no shade in this area.

Chapter 10
DREAM GUIDE TO DISNEY SPRINGS

Welcome to my home away from home! Whilst living in Florida, Disney Springs was my happy place. Whenever I had an afternoon or evening free, I'd be here soaking up the atmosphere.

Disney Springs is a shopping, dining and entertainment village located outside of the parks. It's free to enter and buses take you to and from your resort hotel.

Formally known as Downtown Disney, Disney Springs features; high-street, high-end and exclusive shopping. It has plenty of snack, quick service and table service dining locations. It also has a multiplex cinema, bowling alley, NBC experience and live entertainment nightly.

No matter where you're staying, Disney Springs is worth one or two visits during your holiday. With some of the best eats in the Orlando area, it's well worth your time popping over for an evening.

TOP TIPS

There's so much to see and do at Disney Springs, I could write an entire book on all the places you could experience here. Even if you spent two weeks just at Disney Springs, you still couldn't try it all! Here's some top tips for a visit.

★ **Parking** - First of all, it's FREE! So even if you're staying off-property, there's no reason to hesitate visiting even for an hour or two. Secondly, Disney has employed a digital parking system that will show you how many spaces are free on each level. Not only that, a green beacon will appear over any empty spaces. With an updated road system, it's easy to get in and out of Disney Springs quickly.

★ **Boat Service** - To help you get around, boats service the three main areas of the property. Whilst these services may take longer than walking typically, if you're going from Marketplace to West Side, it'll save you one heck of a walk.

★ **What Can You Get Elsewhere?** - One of the biggest mistakes guests make at Disney Springs, is dining at places they've heard of before. Rainforest Cafe for example is one of the busiest locations but really, you can find one in every major city.

★ **Shopping Mornings** - If it's stores like Sephora, Kate Spade and Zara exciting you to take a trip to Disney Springs, choose to visit in the morning when the stores open at 9am. It's considerably quieter before lunchtime most days.

Dining

If it's food you're after, you'll be spoilt for choice at Disney Springs! With a large variety of quick service and table service options, there's something for every budget and preference. If you're struggling for what to do and know you need to get lunch/dinner, there's a good chance you'll find what you're craving.

Quick Service Dining

These options are incredibly popular at Disney Springs. Whilst they're called 'quick' service, due to the lines at most of these locations - don't expect to be in and out in a flash. Similar to the parks, if you can avoid those peak dining hours, it'll save you a lot of time when you're enjoying your time here. If there's a long line, chances are it's somewhere worth waiting for. Here are my top eats:

Chicken Guy

✦ ✦ ✦ ✦ ✦

By far one of the most popular and affordable options at Disney Springs is Chicken Guy! Serving up the best chicken tenders you'll ever eat and more sauces that you can shake a stick at, this is one of my favourites! Evening's can be pretty busy here so I'd recommend visiting for lunch.

Blaze Pizza

Think Subway but with Pizza. Here you can choose every element of your own pizza! Not only is it incredibly flexible to what each person in your party wants, it's super cheap! You're looking at less that $15 a person here, making it the best for value in my opinion.

D-Luxe Burger

I hope you're ready to have the best burger of your life! It's pricier than other quick service restaurants but it's 100% worth it! Whilst often pretty busy, there's a reason. The line to order often moves pretty slowly. As such, this is a great time to utilise Mobile Order (page 77).

Earl of Sandwich

By far my favourite dining location in Magic Kingdom, this quick service serves New England style home comforts such as Chicken Pot Pie, Lobster Roles and more! Head upstairs for ample seating and a nice chill out from the hustle and bustle of the park.

Table Service Dining

We've got table service options coming out of our ears at Disney Springs! Having tried a lot of them (not all of them) I've picked out some of my favourites. Being true to my statement earlier of trying places you can't find elsewhere, you won't find the cliché visitor locations here.

Jaleo

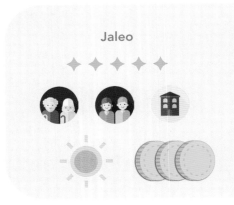

Possibly the freshest tapas I've ever had, if you don't mind trying new foods, Jaleo is a must! The culinary team here starts as early as 4:30am to start prepping the freshest organic food. The exceptional attention to detail is even in the bread, that's flown in from Spain!

Frontera Cocina

I LOVE Mexican food. It's also one of the only things I can cook consistently well. However, not as well as the chefs at Frontera Cocina! If you're looking to try some of the menu before investing in a full meal, consider getting a snack from the quick service window.

Chef Art Smith's Homecomin'

If you like fried chicken and southern style hospitality, look no further than Homecomin'! I had to go back here a couple of times the food and atmosphere was so good! I'd recommend this location for adults who like trying alcoholic beverages.

The Boathouse

Great food and great service. Every single cast member at this location was on it. Everyone greeted us, our server was possibly the best I'd ever had and everyone wished us well when we left. The only downside was waiting for our table and the proximity to other guests.

Snacks & Speciality

Whilst it's great to grab a meal in Disney Springs, there's a couple of fly-by places you simply have to try! There's a lot of small kiosk style eats around the property, so you'll never be far away from a quick snack or drink. However, the two below are places I have down as must-dos.

Sprinkles

Sweet tooth? Well, get ready to try the best cupcake ever! Everyone I've taken here for the first time has had the same look of pure euphoria as they bite into their first frosted Sprinkles cupcake. They even have a cupcake vending machine outside! Salted Caramel's my fave.

Coca-Cola Store

All that eating and shopping might have taken it out of you! Well, there's no better place to chill out than the roof-top bar at the Coca-cola store. This is where you can sample various Coca-Cola products from around the world and just enjoy a sunny day.

Shopping

Welcome to shopaholic heaven! If like me it doesn't take a lot to enable you into a purchase, only take a certain amount of money with you to Disney Springs. Below you'll find some of my favourites and the most popular stores.

⭐ **Sephora** - If you're from the UK and love make-up, I know you're already cracking your neck ready for this store! With a great selection of make-up and skin-care products you can't find everywhere, it's a great place for international visitors to pick up some of those products that are just too expensive to ship home. I have sensitive skin and with me, the advisors know their stuff and can recommend what's right for you.

⭐ **365 Days of Christmas** - If you're up for a bit of festive cheer (no matter the time of year) pop by the Days of Christmas store at the far end of Disney Springs Marketplace. Not only does it smell of festive goodness but you can also find some special ornaments to prep yourself for the Christmas season or even get a bauble personalised.

⭐ **Art of Disney** - Just across the way from the Days of Christmas store is the best place for Disney art and graphic pieces. It's also where you can find the original paintings that are replicated across property. If there's a particular character you or a friend likes, you can get a custom animation done of the character of your choosing. Maybe something special for an upcoming birthday?

⭐ **UNIQLO** - If you're missing some essentials (e.g. vests, t-shirts etc.) this is the place to pick them up at an affordable price. Not only that, they have a great Disney selection! The lines tend to change pretty regularly so if you see something you like then get it! As this store has so much footfall, it can sometimes be difficult to find items in your size.

Chapter 11
DREAM GUIDE TO MORE

By now, you should already know Walt Disney World is big! There's so much fun to be had in your resort hotel and in the parks. However, when you're spending a week, or two in the Orlando area, there's also so much beyond the Disney parks.

In this chapter, I'm going to take you through some of my favourite things to do beyond the parks. A lot of families get into the habit of sticking to what they know. This should helpfully show you what you may be missing out on.

Disney Resorts

Fort Wilderness Campfire - Roast smores by a campfire whilst Chip and Dale host a special sing-along! Then, enjoy a Disney movie on the big open-air screen. As long as it's not due to rain, head to the Meadow Depot area for this FREE experience (smores kits cost about $10). To get to the venue when you arrive at Fort Wilderness, take an internal bus on either the yellow or orange route.

Horses at Fort Wilderness - If anyone in your party likes horses, make time to visit the stables at The Settlement at Fort Wilderness. I recommend going in the afternoon for the chance to speak to the cast members there and maybe even get a tour of the stables. Call ahead for the most up-to-date times.

Hoop-Dee-Doo Musical Revue - The dinner show of all dinner shows! Having been a number of times, this dinner show at Fort Wilderness is well worth your time. Whilst not cheap, it's worth the money! Pro-tip, if you can go at the later show and book a cheaper seat, if the show isn't full, you'll likely get an upgrade.

Fireworks from the Polynesian Village Resort - Just across the Seven Seas Lagoon from Magic Kingdom is the Polynesian. If you fancy seeing some fireworks but not the hustle and bustle of the parks, stop-by not long before firework time at Magic Kingdom and maybe pick-up a Dole Whip from the dedicated kiosk near the main lobby. Alternatively, if you're over 21 and fancy some crazy cocktails, stop-by Trader Sams for something really special!

Grand Floridian Music - Visit Disney's Grand Floridian resort after 4pm for your chance to enjoy the live pianist and band that rotate through the evening. If you'd like a date night, the Grand is the place to be. Adorn some of your fancy attire and see if you can get a reservation at Citricos. Enjoy some cocktails at the Enchanted Rose bar if you really want to push the boat out!

River Roost - Located at Port Orleans Riverside, on select nights through the week, you can enjoy a piano show unlike any other. Most popular with regulars of the resort, you'll want to get there ahead of the show starting to be even in the chance of scoring a table. Even if you're not staying at the resort, it's something fun for the whole family and the quick service there is amazing!

Water Parks

In Orlando, you've got four main water parks to choose from. At Disney, you'll find Typhoon Lagoon and Blizzard Beach. Sea World runs Aquatica and at Universal, you've got Volcano Bay. If you had to choose from one and you're going to be paying for your entry, I'd recommend Volcano Bay as it'd by far my favourite.

However, if you're visiting Disney and have their water parks included in your ticket, I don't think it's worth paying extra to go to other water parks. Here are some tips to help you get the most out of whichever water park you go to.

⭐ **Towels** - It costs to rent towels at the water parks. With that in mind, if you're staying at a Disney resort hotel, stop-by your pool to pick-up some complimentary towels and take them with you.

⭐ **Go Early** - Especially if visiting the new Volcano Bay water park at Universal, go for opening. Not only do they sometimes reach capacity but the heat will be much kinder to your feet as you walk about the park.

⭐ **Slides** - If you're visiting Blizzard Beach in particular, know some of the slides aren't the most comfortable. The grooves in the slide tend to hurt after a while and so I mostly stick to the rubber ring or mat slides.

⭐ **Hydrate** - It's so important to drink water at the water parks. As you're in and out of water, you can sometimes forget how hot it really is. Especially when you're climbing stairs and swimming all day!

⭐ **MagicBands** - If you haven't linked a credit card to your MagicBand, a water park day is a good day to do it. As you can buy food, drinks and save your Photopass photos with your band, it'll save you having to go into the locker.

Orlando Dining

With Orlando attracting millions of visitors annually, there are plenty of places to eat outside of Disney!

If you want to go off property one night, maybe to save a dining credit for a signature location or you're renting a villa, these are some of my favourite off property restaurants.

⭐ **Cheesecake Factory** - Not far from Universal is Mall at Millennia. There you'll find the Cheesecake Factory. It's probably the biggest menu you'll ever find and the portions are crazy! Just note the wait is normally an hour.

⭐ **BJ's Brewhouse** - If you want a lot of choice but don't want to stray too far from Disney, BJ's is the place for you. This was a typical haunt for my colleagues and I after a long day at work. Lots of choice and not too pricey.

⭐ **Saffron Indian Cuisine** - For us Brits, an indian curry is as British as Fish & Chips. I made it one of my missions to find a decent curry in Orlando and I believe I found it! The papadams miss the mark but everything else is ace.

⭐ **Sweet Tomatoes** - For a lunch that's affordable and healthy, consider Sweet Tomatoes. Located just beyond Disney Springs (currently), it's an all you care to eat salad and hot food buffet.

⭐ **Panera Bread** - My personal favourite destination for breakfast or lunch off property. With soups in bread bowls, hot sandwiches and a great bakery selection, it's affordable and different from locations in Disney.

Universal Studios

Whilst beyond the gates of Disney, Universal Orlando Resort is worth at least one of your days if you've never been to Florida before or if you've been to Disney a couple of times. My advice for a visit to Universal, is to not compare it to Disney like-for-like. If you like thrills and 3D, you're bound to have a great day at their two theme parks.

Getting There - If you're staying at Disney, it can often be a tricky business knowing exactly how to get to Universal. In my experience, I've found ride share services like Lyft and Uber are the most convenient and the most affordable.

PRO TIP

Order your ride share to and from one of Universal's hotels (especially during busy times). You'll have a much more pleasant experience entering/ leaving the resort this way.

Dining - I personally struggle to find food I really love at Universal (quick service especially). A lot of people go for the Harry Potter themed locations but the food isn't amazing in my opinion. My advice is to venture onto City Walk about lunch time and have your main meal there. Hard Rock Cafe is one of my favourites, as is Bubba Gump's and Panda Express.

Express Pass - Universal doesn't have a complimentary fast pass service. With that, do I think their paid express pass is worth it? If you're there for one day and it's busy, sure! Outside of that, I personally wouldn't opt for it.

Lockers - It's important to know ahead of time, you can't take bags on most attractions at Universal. With that in mind - if you can survive with just things in your pockets, do! A couple of roller coasters require you to empty your pockets and they have plenty of small lockers for pocket-like items, but few for family bags. You'll save yourself a lot of hassle.

Motion Sickness - If like me, you find motion simulators a little 'much,' really consider whether a ride is suitable for you. With so many rides featuring motion simulators and 3D, one ride could ruin your day if it makes you feel unwell. The worst offenders for me are The Simpsons Ride, Transformers: The Ride, Skull Island: Reign of Kong and Spider-man: The Ride.

2 Park Pass - Can you do two parks in one day? Yes. Should you? Yes. You can spend a number of days in Universal but if you just want to 'do it,' you'll easily be able to catch the highlights in both parks with a one day, 2 park ticket.

Hagrid's Motorbike Adventure - Still unbeaten as my favourite ride/roller coaster in the whole world, this is the world's first story coaster. Using state-of-the-art technology, seven launches and multiple systems, this is one attraction you will not want to miss (no matter how long the wait is)!

Water Rides - The water rides at Universal will get you wet. VERY wet. With that in mind, dress accordingly or bring a change of clothes to avoid squelching for the resort of the day.

PRO TIP

Buy your tickets online and collect from a will-call kiosk to save time. If needing to purchase at the gate, do so at Islands of Adventure.

Local Attractions

Universal and Disney is what most people will think of when visiting the Orlando area. There are however plenty of day-out attractions near-by!

I've spent at least one day at each of these attractions but these are just my views. Having not spent lots of time there, this is what I found in my day there and your day may differ.

Sea World - For me, the roller coasters were a little too intense for even my tastes and the zoo/aquarium side of the park wasn't to my liking. The park's quality in terms of service, facilities and theming has slipped over the years and I'm sorry to say I don't think it's worth the entry fee right now.

I don't buy the whole Black Fish documentary belief that Sea World is evil - I actually got to see some of the rehabilitation and rescue work they do and was incredibly impressed. The park just doesn't deliver against what I'd like.

PRO TIP

If you're staying at Disney and want to rent a car for a day or two, you can do so at the Swan and Dolphin resort next to Disney's Boardwalk.

Kennedy Space Center - Bit of a drive but if you're as into space as I am, it's worth the trip and entry fee.

It's more of a museum than an attraction but I loved seeing the work that goes into the NASA space program and would go again if I had the time.

Legoland Florida - If you've got little ones below the age of 12, I'd say Legoland is a must do for you!

I had the BEST time here (mainly because I'm a big kid). The park right now isn't too busy but it's clean, the staff are friendly and you really get your money's worth.

A ride share to the park from Disney will set you back about $50 but split between a few of you, doesn't work out too bad when you consider the distance.

The rides are targeted at the younger guests but the roller coasters are still enjoyable for adults. I'd consider this more of a local park, so do your best to go on a weekday and whilst the local schools are not on a break.

We didn't wait more than 15 minutes for a ride all day when we went on an off-peak Monday.

FUN FACT

Legoland Florida is built on the former location of the infamous Florida attraction, Cypress Gardens.

Busch Gardens Tampa Bay - Another one that's a drive from the Orlando area but if you like roller coasters, you won't be disappointed!

Whilst part of the Sea World company, the theme park side of Busch Gardens is better than Sea World in my opinion. There's plenty of attractions and similar to Legoland, if you can go on an off-peak weekday, you likely won't have to wait long for anything.

Orlando i360 - Located on International Drive, this is a multi-attraction and dining complex featuring Madame Tussauds, SeaLife and the Orlando Eye.

It's a little touristy for my liking (and priced as such) but it's a nice stop-off. Especially if you're looking for something different and you're staying off Disney property.

Tours

I love learning about how the Disney parks operate. I find it so interesting to see how Walt's ideas materialised into what we get to enjoy today.

Across property are a variety of tours that will allow you to see everything from how the Christmas decorations come to life, to how Disney look after the animals at Animal Kingdom.

Whilst the tours can be pricey, I'd say they're worth every penny for the service and experience. You can book a tour via the main booking line which is currently +1 407-939-8687.

My favourite tours include:

Keys to the Kingdom - An all day tour that allows you to see how Magic Kingdom operates behind the scenes.

Be warned, this is a long walking tour! On the tour you'll get to see inside the utilidoor (the tunnels underneath Magic Kingdom that cast members use to get around), enjoy a couple of rides with your tour guide and it includes a quick service lunch.

Marceline to Magic - Probably the best value tour, this Magic Kingdom walking tour shows you how Walt went from Marceline, Missouri to creating the world of Disney we enjoy today.

This lasts approximately three hours and will allow you to see how the ghosts in Haunted Mansion work, as well as a guided tour of Main Street U.S.A. and a ride on Carousel of Progress.

Wilk Africa Trek - One of the best things I've ever done in my life! Not only are the cast that conduct this tour beyond amazing, the tour itself offers you the chance to rope bridge (weather permitting) over Nile Crocodile, learn about animals and dine in the middle of the savannah!

If you choose to do this tour and like me, there's a few things you don't like to eat (e.g. shellfish), mention this when checking in for your tour. Your meal out on the Savannah has to be prepared in advance.

Boating - Not exactly a tour but from select Walt Disney World hotels, you can take a small speedboat or even a pontoon out on the lakes around Walt Disney World.

I'd recommend packing a picnic and taking a pontoon out from the Grand Floridian. It's a nice way to explore both Bay Lake and Seven Seas Lagoon. You don't need any qualifications or boating experience, you'll be given a demonstration before setting off and lifeguards are on-hand around the lakes.

Wanyama Safari - Run at Animal Kingdom Lodge, this is a tour for those of you looking to enjoy some fine dining as well as a guided safari.

I'd say this tour is on the more luxurious side and is a lot more sociable than the other tours I've experienced. Your group are made to feel like one big family as you enjoy a 45-60 minute tour of the savannahs at the lodge, followed by a family-style meal at Jiko.

Dessert Parties

To enhance your trip, you may want to consider a dessert party! Normally attached to a fireworks show, these ticketed experiences allow you to indulge in an all-you-care-to-enjoy buffet (mainly consisting of desserts) and unlimited beer, wine, cocktails, mocktails and soft drinks. Prices for dessert parties vary but $60-100 is a good guide.

Are they worth the money? Well, it depends on what you're hoping to get out of them. If you're looking for a guaranteed good view of a show you haven't seen before, then yes, they're worth their weight in gold. If however you're looking for a buffet that'll replace your evening meal, it may be worth considering an alternative.

In my experience, dessert parties are something special. If you're celebrating someone's birthday, an anniversary, engagement etc. Then a dessert party is a great way to mark the occasion. To book a dessert party, call:

+1 407 WDW-PLAY (+1 407 939 7529)

FUN FACT

The grandmother animatronic in the Haunted Mansion Ballroom is a duplicate of the Carousel of Progress one.

Outlets & Malls

If you're looking for retail therapy, Orlando's got you covered! From malls showcasing only the finest of designer labels, to outlets that'll help you find a mega deal, you can shop until you drop.

In fact, on every trip I take to Disney, I'll put aside at least one day for going shopping. Mainly as I can save a pretty penny buying my clothes state-side.

⭐ **Mall at Millennia** - Located near Universal Studios, this mall is best for designer stores (full price).

⭐ **Florida Mall** - Ideal for a more varied shopping experience, you'll find more choice here if you're looking to kill some time.

⭐ **Premium Outlets: Vineland Avenue** - Not too far from Disney, this outlet mall is where I'd recommend going at least once on your trip. Mainly for Character Warehouse (a discounted Disney Parks merchandise store) but also for Pop-Bar, an amazing frozen yogurt lolly stand that is everything!

Ticketed Events

Throughout the year, Disney will often host exclusive ticketed events. These vary from Early Morning events that allow you to ride a select number of attractions and enjoy a breakfast, right through to a Christmas Party that covers the whole of Magic Kingdom! Ticketed events can be a great way to enhance your holiday but some of them aren't always worth the money. Depending on what you want to get out of your event, depends on whether it's worth the money for you.

Book by calling: +1 407 WDW-PLAY (+1 407 939 7529)

Early Morning Magic

Whilst not run as often, these are by far my favourite ticketed events. I'm a morning person and I love rides! For me, there's a lot of value in being able to walk on a bunch of attractions.

I think Early Morning Magic events are worth the money (Approx $75) and make for a great first day if you've got jet lag and time difference on your side.

After Hours

Similar to Early Morning Magic, After Hours events give you the chance to enjoy little to no waits on most attractions, snacks and refreshments, with addition of exclusive character meet & greets. Villains After Hours is probably the best of these events.

Mickey's Not So Scary Halloween Party

Tickets cost approximately $100 per person and in my opinion, Mickey's Not So Scary has decreased in value each year. The event is often oversold which makes Magic Kingdom busier than it is during the day. However, if you're looking for an opportunity to dress-up as your favourite Disney character, go trick-or-treating and maybe meet some characters in their Halloween costumes, I think you'd really enjoy this party. Candy is unlimited and free, the event also features an exclusive parade, castle show and fireworks.

> # PRO TIP
>
> If attending Mickey's Not So Scary Halloween Party or Mickey's Very Merry Christmas Party, I don't recommend going to the first showing of the parade or shows. The second showing, is always quieter! However, if rain is forecast, forget I said that! Shows and parades can be cancelled if it rains. If a lot gets cancelled, stop-by guest services.

Mickey's Very Merry Christmas Party

Not dissimilar from Mickey's Not So Scary in terms of pricing and offerings, I personally prefer the Christmas party. The parade is something very special and the castle lighting ceremony is probably one of my favourite festive things to do anywhere! In place of candy, is unlimited cookies and hot chocolate.

> # PRO TIP
>
> If you're visiting Walt Disney World during a time when there's multiple ticketed events at Magic Kingdom (e.g. Halloween or Christmas), avoid going to Magic Kingdom on non-party days. As tempting as it may be to try and see Happily Ever After, the park will be more than busy! I'd instead visit in the morning of a party day to enjoy a quieter park day.

Index

Acknowledgements

Walt Disney World for me, is my home away from home. Writing this special edition has been very exciting and I hope you've enjoyed using it to plan your trip to Disney. I do, however, have some pillars in my life to thank for making this Dream Guide possible.

This guide wouldn't be as colourful as it is without my dear friend and partner in crime, Gary C. Whilst on our trips to Disney, Gary took the time to photograph everything that could possibly be needed for this book. So to Gary, I thank you. A friend like Gary comes along but once in a lifetime. I'm forever grateful for his support, kindness and humour that make even the darkest day bright. I'd also like to thank him for always being himself and thus creating everlasting moments of tomfoolery for the world to enjoy in the vlogs (moo moo sharoo).

To my Mum and stepdad, I thank you for being there when I need someone to bounce an idea off. For helping guide and support my decisions, even when my decisions weren't exactly what you wanted. Without your loving support, I wouldn't be publishing my fourth book and the managing director of my own company. Thank you for being there and for making me the man I am today.

Last but not least, to lovely you. You were kind enough to buy or ask for this Dream Guide. You've entrusted me to advise you on something as personal as a family holiday and I can't thank you enough!

From watching my vlogs to now reading my words, I appreciate your support and for choosing me, to be part of your Disney adventure. I wish you, your family and/or your friends, the most magical time in Disney. May you live out your biggest dreams and find everlasting happiness in the place we call home.

Other Books by Adam Hattan

Dream Guide: An Unofficial Guide to Disney Cruise Line

Get ready to sail away with Disney Cruise Line and plan your dream cruise with Adam Hattan's unofficial guidebook. From helping you choose the itinerary, cabin and season that's right for you, right down to helping you get the most of your Disney Cruise.

Available at Amazon UK and www.adamhattan.com/books

Dream Planner: A Planner for Your Dream Walt Disney World Holiday

It's time to plan your dream Walt Disney World holiday! With so much to see and do, it's essential to have a plan of which park you're going to, where you'd like to dine and which attractions are your priority. This planner is where you can organise all of those plans!

Available at Amazon UK and www.adamhattan.com/books